By
Peggy A. Hogg
and
Dr. Robert J. Berndt

Grooming and Showing Toy Dogs

Cover Design by
Bruce Parker

Edited by
William W. Denlinger
and
R. Annabel Rathman

DENLINGER'S
Box 76, Fairfax, Virginia 22030

Copyright © 1976

International Standard Book Number: 0-87714-035-9

Library of Congress Catalog Card Number: 75-41981

Grooming and Showing Toy Dogs is designed as a manual for the novice dog show exhibitor. The advice offered here is of a practical nature and is the result of years of first-hand experience gained by the Authors while breeding and showing Toy dogs. It is hoped that this book will save other exhibitors from some of the difficulties encountered by the Authors while they were learning about the various breeds.

Chapters 1, 2, and 8 are pertinent to the exhibitors of all Toy dogs, while Chapters 3 through 7 deal with specific breeds. The Authors suggest that the reader should eventually read all chapters. Since not all dogs of any particular breed are completely typical, it is necessary at times to try different techniques of grooming that may not be normal for that breed. It is quite possible to adapt and to modify grooming techniques for one breed to dogs of another breed.

It is not possible to express gratitude to every individual who made a suggestion that eventually was included in this book. Recognition should, however, be given to all those who furnished photographs. Their sharing of these pictures has made it possible to present a panorama of winning Toy dogs in all Toy breeds.

We do wish to offer special thanks to Mrs. Nancy Cutler of Cutler's Poodles and to Max and Marie Hurd of Hurd's Chihuahuas for their specific contributions to the original manuscript.

P. A. H.
R. J. B.

Foreword

The Authors, Mrs. Peggy A. Hogg and Dr. Robert J. Berndt.

Contents

Left to right, Ch. Coolaroo
Dame Wintiki, Ch. Siltis Joy
Boy, and Ch. Siltis Blu Dimon
Deb. This study shows the
proper grooming of the head
and feet of the Silky Terrier.

When the word "conditioning" is used in connection with the raising of dogs, it describes those procedures which are employed to maintain a dog in the optimum state of health. The areas that would be important under such a system are the maintenance of high standards of health, the feeding of a scientifically balanced diet, and the establishment of a regular program of exercise. While the formality and detail of any such system is a matter of personal taste, these three areas are of universal importance and must be included whether it is in the raising of a single family pet or in the maintenance of a large kennel of show dogs.

Greater care must be given to the conditioning of the show dog, not necessarily because he represents a larger investment of money, but because he is forced into situations that are potentially much more damaging to his general health. Show dogs are constantly being transported from one part of the country to another, traveling hundreds of miles each week to maintain a show schedule. Traveling is hard on the dog, for it disrupts the normal rhythm and routine of his life. He is constantly required to make adjustments and to adapt to new conditions. In addition to the physical strain of travel, there is also the breaking of the routine for sleeping and eating. While a dog may be sleeping in the same crate whether he is at home or on the road, the situation is still not entirely the same. The comfort and security of the home kennel do not exist either in a show building or in a motel. There are always many new and strange noises that disturb the dog's rest. Even while he is sleeping, he is not sleeping so well nor so soundly as he does at home. In addition, his rest is constantly disturbed during the night with the arrival of each new exhibitor. It takes a considerable period of time for some dogs to adjust to the nervous strain as well as to the physical strain of being a show dog. Some dogs, in fact, never do make an adequate adjustment and are forced to retire from a show career.

Traveling in a small crate is also physically exhausting to dogs. The motion of the car or the airplane, the noise and the fumes on the highway—all add to the physical discomfort. Even after arriving at the relative calm and quiet of the show site, the dog is somewhat stiff from his confinement. He does not have the advantage of limbering up as he could at home, for the exercise pen is so much smaller than his kennel run or home exercise yard. This is an espe-

Chapter 1

Conditioning the Toy Dog

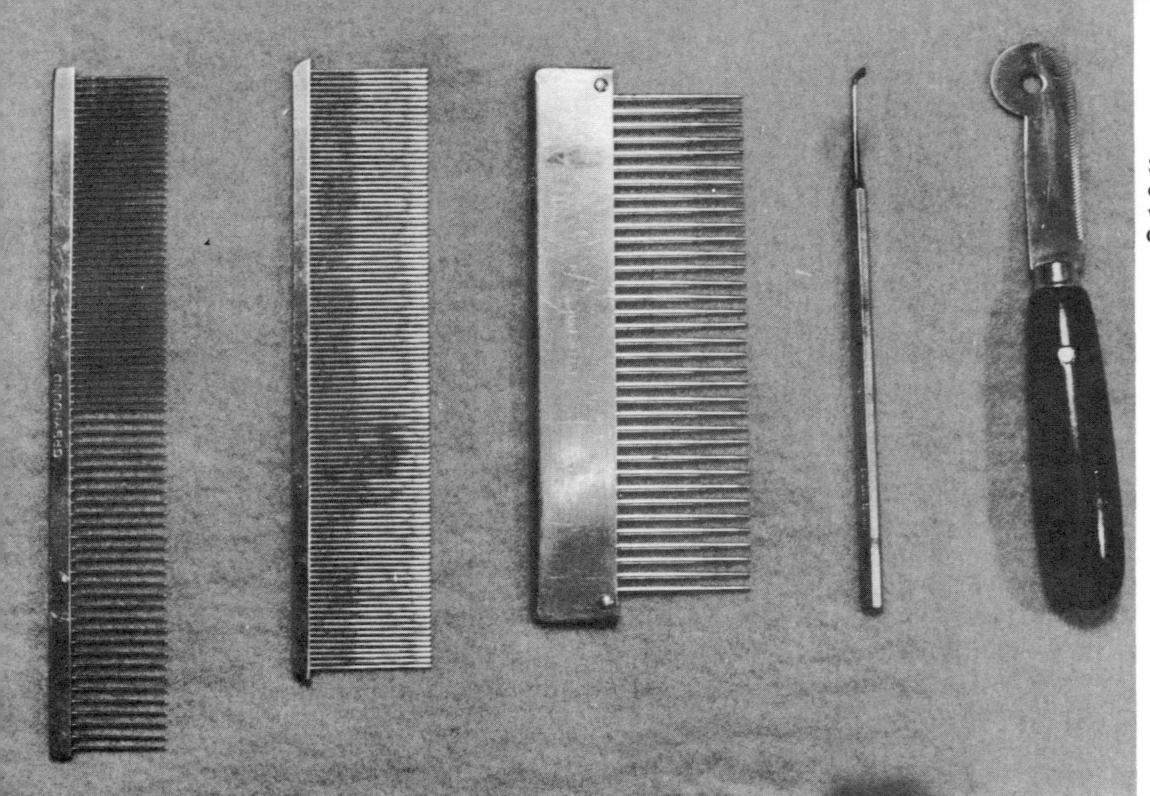

Several types of combs, a dental pick, and a stripper which is used on the Brussels Griffon.

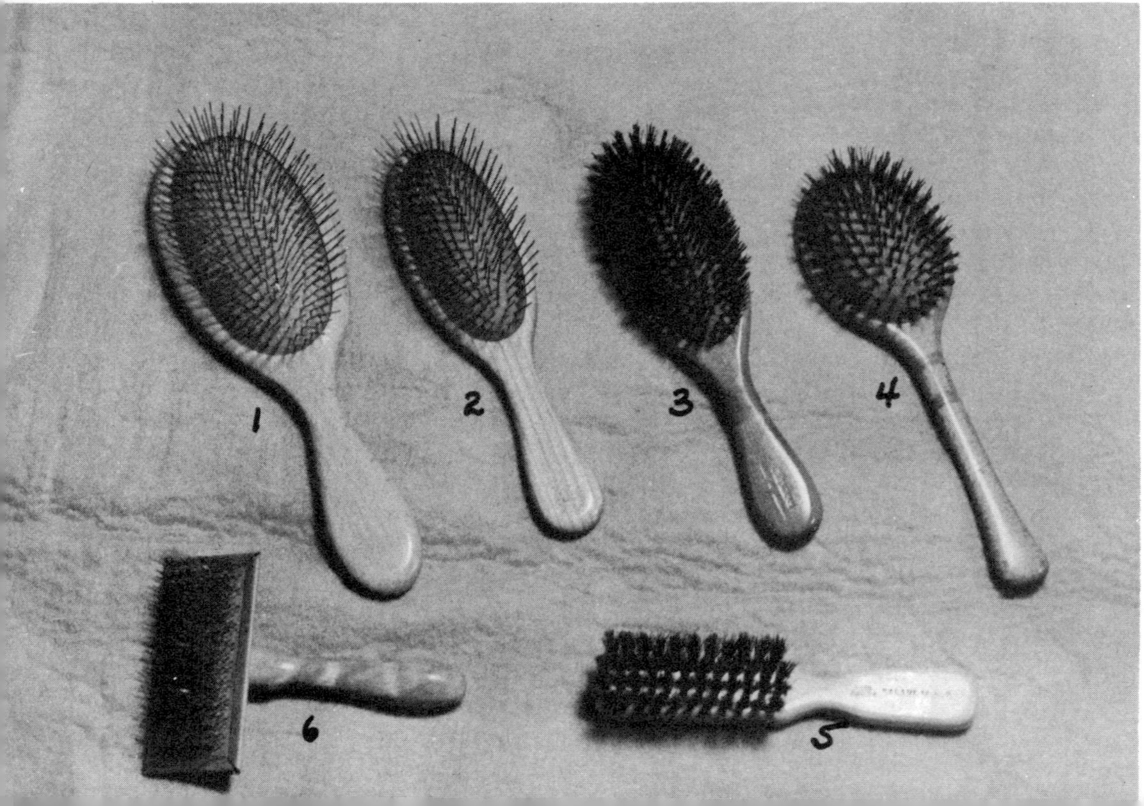

A selection of grooming brushes. Numbers 1 and 2 are pin brushes; 3, 4, and 5 are natural-bristle brushes; and 6 is a slicker brush.

cially serious problem for the very large dogs. The Toy dog can usually get adequate exercise at the shows in large exercise pens or in the areas around the show buildings when he is walked by his handler and allowed to limber up. Large dogs really require a good deal of extra running upon arriving at the show.

To keep physical discomfort to the absolute minimum, it is wise for the handler to carry drinking water for the dog from his home kennel. This will eliminate the possibility of upsetting the dog's stomach with a change in water. Since canned or packaged food is always brought from home, the feeding ritual itself would appear to present no additional problem. Feeding on the road may become a concern, however, for a nervous dog who is accustomed to eating in the quiet of his own kennel run. He may elect not to eat at all on the road and will have to be force-fed in order to maintain his proper body weight. This seems to be a problem which is seen most frequently in the novice dog who is just starting his show career. It can, however, be a problem even with a seasoned "Specials" dog who is a finicky eater. Force-feeding would also be a necessity in this situation.

The aforementioned areas of concern exist for the show dog in addition to those general problems that exist for all dogs—pet or show. General conditions of health, diet, and exercise must be watched constantly to prevent a lowering of standards that would result in a serious health problem for the dog.

General Health of the Toy Dog

Preventive medicine is the means of maintaining good health that should be practiced by a show kennel. It is kinder to the dog and is a practical method of ensuring that he will be available for showing for extended periods of time. Routine checks for parasites and the maintenance of inoculations are essential not only for the show dogs but also for family pets. Many handlers and owners of show dogs provide inoculations twice a year in order to keep protection at the highest possible levels.

There are three serious diseases to which dogs are susceptible. They are distemper, hepatitis, and leptospirosis. These diseases are serious because they are frequently fatal. For-

tunately, there are effective inoculations against all three.

External parasites such as fleas and ticks may not be of such great concern as the above-mentioned diseases, but they are extremely annoying to the dog. While lice can also be a problem for dogs, they are not so common since they usually exist only when sanitary conditions are extremely poor in the kennel area. Fleas and ticks are present, however, in almost all parts of the country during warm weather. They are easy to pick up and sometimes quite difficult to eliminate, especially in the case of long-coated dogs. Fleas and ticks not only are annoying to the dog but also are capable of causing a dog to become infested with worms and they sometimes transmit diseases.

The simple rule for practicing preventive medicine is to consult the veterinarian whenever there is the least question concerning any condition of the dog. This is especially true in the case of the various types of diseases of the skin or conditions that result from the presence of seasonal irritants. All of these problems should be treated promptly in order to prevent the development of a chronic condition which not only can ruin a show coat, but also can become detrimental to the over-all health of the dog.

Physical Problems of Toy Dogs

In addition to the common illnesses and diseases that affect dogs in general, Toy dogs have a number of physical problems that are peculiar to them. They also have a few advantages over certain other classes of dogs.

Many of the special problems affecting Toy dogs result from their having been bred down to their present size. Toy dogs are really a creation of man and not the end-product of a series of natural and environmental developments. Most of the small dogs were bred to reduce their size to try to turn a utilitarian working animal into an amusing house pet. By breeding ever-smaller specimens, man has had to be willing to accept certain characteristics which are now well established in nearly all of the Toy breeds.

Mouths are of concern for most Toy breeds. In breeding ever-smaller heads, the muzzle became quite small. The teeth were reduced in size, but could go only so small. As a result, the number of teeth decreased or the teeth came in crooked. The whole genetic pattern became disturbed, and frequently double rows of very tiny teeth appear. The quantity of teeth is one problem, but the quality of the teeth is also of concern. The tiny teeth frequently do not have sufficient thickness of enamel to protect them and as a result they decay and must be removed when the dog is still quite young. While this problem may exist in larger dogs, it is the exception rather than the rule. The show careers of many Toy dogs have been cut short because of poor teeth.

With the reduction of size of the dog, there was an accompanying reduction of muscle. This is evident in many Toy dogs, and it is especially easy to see in hind leg structure. The patella, or kneecap, is not sufficiently anchored with muscle and tendon to serve the leg to its best advantage. The result of this physical weakness is a poor rear movement and general weakness of the hindquarters. In some cases exercise will help the condition, but, if the case is a severe one, exercise will only compound the discomfort to the dog.

Heartworms are much more serious in the Toy dog than in the larger dogs. The prognosis for heartworms is very poor. Since everything in the Toy dog is in miniature, the methods that are effective for large dogs cannot work for Toys. The blood vessels are usually smaller than the heartworm itself so that once the worm is lodged in the heart it cannot be eliminated. It cannot be passed even if it can be destroyed in the heart. The situation is really a hopeless one. This is why great care must be given to preventive medical treatment in this area.

The last area of major concern for the small dogs is in their breeding and whelping. Breeding of Toy dogs must sometimes be done artificially because of physical obstructions in the bitch or the lack of stamina on the part of the stud. Artificial insemination is never as effective as a natural breeding. There is a higher rate of not conceiving when bitches are bred artificially. Whelping is also a problem when the pelvis is very small or when the puppy is just an ounce or two larger than normal.

Litter size in Toy dogs is frequently limited to one or two puppies. This requires a kennel owner to keep a larger number of brood bitches. Since a Toy bitch may produce only six or eight puppies in her lifetime, it is difficult to establish quantity show records for leading sires or dams. In larger breeds a bitch can deliver in one litter what a Toy bitch might produce during her entire breeding lifetime.

Physical Advantages of the Toy Dog

The diminutive size has caused some physical problems for the Toy dog, but it has also spared him from others. Hip dysplasia, the curse of the large dog, is nonexistent in Toy breeds. The lack of excessive body weight spares the hip joints the added strain that results in a dysplastic dog.

Since most Toy dogs are bred to have short backs, they do not have the spinal problems that the longer, heavier dogs have. The exceptionally short-backed dog, while he will not have a back problem, may have a gaiting problem, since his stride will be proportionately long and the movement of the hind legs will crowd the front legs. He will, in this case, be forced to gait at a slight angle to avoid stepping on his own front heels.

Since Toy dogs do not carry excessive weight, there is no added strain to their hearts, and as a result, they are the longest lived of all dogs. Small dogs living into their teens is really the average today, whereas the larger, heavier dogs may have a life span of only six to eight years.

While progressive retinal atrophy, or PRA, is of great concern for some of the larger breeds, it seems to be of little concern at present for Toy dogs. There have, of course, been isolated cases, but the bulk of the evidence is that the Toys have been spared.

Size has also led to more experimental breeding. This is seen in the willingness of owners to fly their bitches all over the country to be bred to a particular stud. The cost and ease of shipping small dogs contribute to this. Many owners of large dogs are discouraged by the cost and inconvenience of shipping.

Toy dogs have been growing in popularity during the past few years and will continue to become more popular—to the disadvantage of larger breeds. Changing patterns of living for dog owners, decreasing amounts of physical space for both dog and man, and spiraling costs of maintaining numbers of large dogs will make Toy dogs especially attractive in years to come.

Diet

The scientific feeding of dogs today is much easier than at any time in the past. This is the result of the research that has been undertaken by companies that produce food for animals. During the past few years much money has been spent on the study of animal nutrition, especially that of the dog. Research in animal nutrition is, in fact, much further advanced than that of man.

Scientifically produced commercial products are available in a variety of packaging options. Claims are made that a particular product is all that a dog will need. The nutritional values may be adequate, but dogs, like people, need sufficient variety to make meals interesting.

Dry bulk dog food is manufactured under a number of commercial labels. Even though these products appear similar, the real differences can be detected by studying the labels for ingredients. The kennel owner may have to experiment to discover just which products give the best results for the costs. Canned dog food also comes in a variety of flavors. There is pure meat, meat and meat by-products, and meat and a maximum of cereals. Studying the labels of these canned meat products is of great importance, for some of them are truly non-nutritional and merely supply bulk to the diet.

The newest product on the market is the cellophane-packaged high protein concentrated foods which have little moisture content. These foods come in a variety of forms imitating ground hamburger or chopped meat. They usually do not supply the needed bulk to the diet and must, therefore, be supplemented with a bulk type food.

Many large kennels prefer to mix their own food, using as a base the dry bulk food. This is moistened and then is enriched with either cooked hamburger or chicken. Fat stewing-type chicken can be pressure cooked and ground and added to the food. This gives a particularly rich diet. Feed costs must be kept in line in a large kennel where uneaten food can run up expenses in a very brief period of time. To achieve maximum efficiency of food, the diet must not only be nutritional, but also have a taste appealing to the dog. Uneaten food, no matter how nutritional it is, represents a loss of money to the kennel operator and a loss of energy for the dog.

Each dog owner, after a few years, is sure that he has discovered the key to proper nutrition because he has a fat dog. Weight does not, however, always mean a healthy dog. Some dogs that appear healthy, for example, seem to

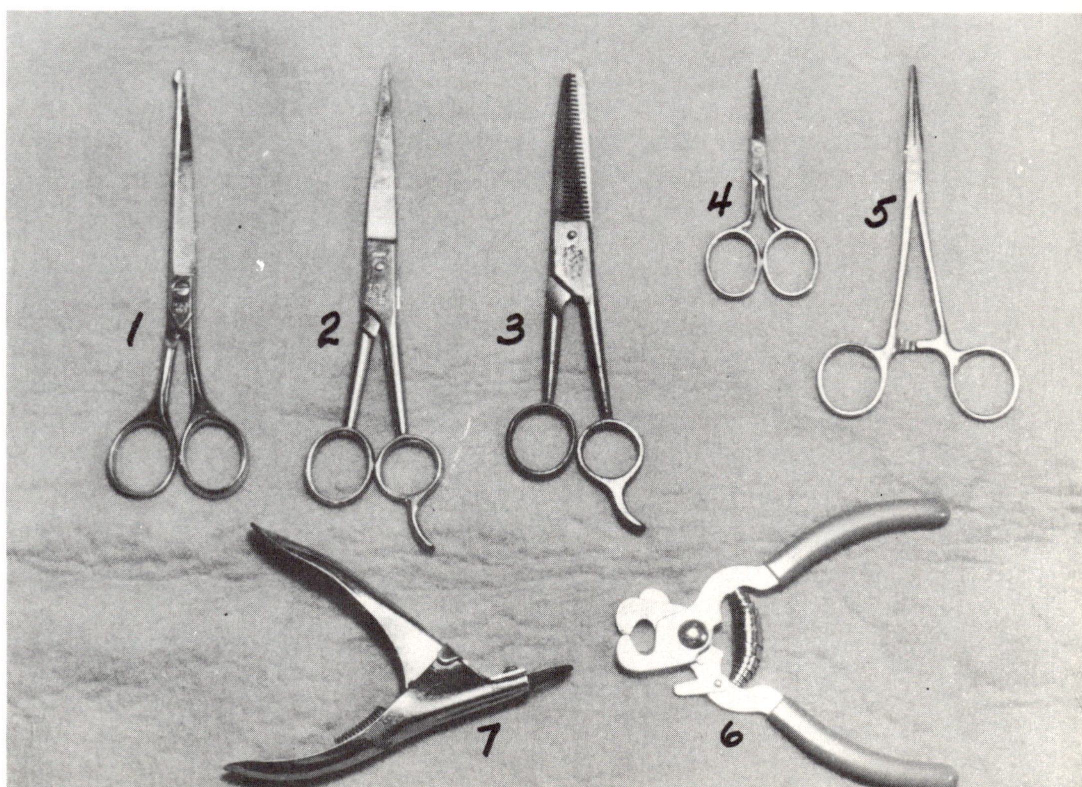

Number 1 is a curved, blunt nose scissors used for under lines; 2, straight scissors used on Poodle packs; 3, thinning shears; 4, curved, blunt nose scissors used to trim whiskers; 5, hemostat used for pulling hair from the ear; and 6 and 7, nail trimmers.

be susceptible to colds and other minor maladies. An improved diet can sometimes be beneficial in helping to correct this problem.

If pure canned meat is to be used, it should be used sparingly. Too much meat is not good for the dog. The pure canned meat should be mixed with the bulk food or with some of the packaged concentrates. If, on the other hand, canned meat products contain cereals and other non-meat products, larger portions may be needed. One diet plan that has proved successful is a combination of pure meat and a concentrated product in a one to four ratio, supplemented with a dry or moistened bulk food for roughage. A spoonful of polyunsaturated oil can be added to this to ensure a balanced diet. Oil added to the food aids in the maintenance of a good coat—one that will have a healthy sheen to it.

For a large kennel, this diet would be an expensive feeding program; but for the family show dog, it provides a well-balanced diet that takes full advantage of present-day research in animal nutrition.

The Kennel Area

Cleanliness of the kennel area is of prime importance in the general conditioning of the dog. Standards of hygiene must be maintained at high levels at all times. Not only must the dog be kept physically clean, but also his kennel and his exercise area must be maintained in the best of all possible conditions. The kenneling area itself should be scrubbed thoroughly every day and disinfected regularly with a highly effective chemical decontaminant. Accumulated dirt and stain in corners and crevices serve as the breeding ground for diseases which can attack the dog. It is important to keep the kennel walls painted with a scrubbable paint to keep them as nonporous as possible. An ideal construction material for a kennel is glazed ceramic tile bricks which can be scrubbed with strong disinfectants that will destroy germs. It must be remembered, however, that tile construction does have its own set of problems in that the cement or grouting in between the tiles is of a porous nature and can be difficult to keep germfree.

Exercise Areas

The exercise yard is the area of greatest concern, for it is by far the most difficult to sterilize. Many types of surfaces are used in exercise yards, but they all have problems to one degree or another. Perhaps the most common surface covering for an exercise yard is crushed gravel. This is a satisfactory surface, for it serves to keep the dog out of the mud and it is relatively easy to scoop up droppings from the stones. In addition, the urine runs through easily, keeping it off the dog's feet. The dirt under the gravel, however, does serve as a breeding ground for parasites. This problem can, and should, be treated on a regular basis. One effective treatment for gravel exercise yards is an application of dry lime. The lime is sprinkled lightly over the entire yard and then washed through the gravel with a hose. Sufficient water should be used to ensure that the top surface is free of any residue, and also to ensure that the lime solution reaches the dirt underneath where the parasites are.

Some kennels prefer to use concrete patio blocks as a substitute for the crushed gravel. And others even use them in addition to the gravel. There should be a base on which the blocks rest. This could be either sand or gravel. Sand is a very harsh material where long-coated dogs are involved, but it does give good drainage. It is harder to pick up droppings from the patio blocks than from the bare gravel but it can be done. The biggest problem with patio blocks is keeping them sterilized. The low density and the porosity of the surface permit accumulations to build up.

Another treatment for exercise yards is to pave the entire surface with concrete. If the surface of the concrete is polished while it is drying, it will have a finish that will be easy to keep clean, but it will also have a surface that is too smooth for the dog to run on. A brushed concrete finish is best for the dog but is much more difficult to keep sterilized. A concrete surface can easily be scrubbed down with hot water and soap on a daily basis, which should help prevent any build-up that could cause problems. The pitch of the runs should be laid out very carefully to make sure that there is proper drainage which allows the runs to dry quickly. One problem with concrete runs is that urine does not disappear rapidly enough, which makes it possible for the dog to run through it. This will quickly accumulate and form a sticky substance on the dog's feet, or in the case of a long-coated dog, on the tips of the hair. Such accumulations must be carefully washed away before grooming can be attempted or the hair ends will be damaged.

Many kennels maintain a large fenced running area adjacent to the regular individual kennel runs. In most cases this is covered with grass. This gives the dog an opportunity to exercise on a softer material and will help to adjust the show dog to the grass rings he will encounter at outdoor shows. These grass areas cannot be used in rainy weather if the dog is one of the longer coated varieties, for romping dogs can turn a wet grassy area into a mud field very rapidly. There is also the serious problem of keeping a grass covered area sterilized. Any chemical strong enough to destroy parasites and their eggs would also destroy the grass. In northern areas where there is severe ground freezing during several weeks of the year, the problem is less serious. In areas where the temperature is moderate all year, care must be taken to keep contaminated dogs out of an area where their condition might cause a problem for other dogs.

Large exercise areas are of great importance for the overall development of the dog. For any dog to develop and to maintain the proper musculature, he must have a large area in which he can run freely. The relationship between muscle and bone is important in maintaining a well-balanced specimen. A dog with substantial bone and small muscles would not be a good representative of any breed. Proper muscle tone can only be achieved when the dog is allowed to exercise in a rather free fashion. In some of the larger breeds, especially the Working and the Sporting Dogs, a regular routine of planned exercise is undertaken. One of the more popular methods of regimented exercise is for the handler to run the dogs while riding a bicycle. Some of the larger dogs are even led from the tailgate of a station wagon. These dogs are regularly run three, four, or even five miles a day to maintain muscle tone.

One of the newer pieces of equipment that can be seen in larger kennels today is the mechanical exerciser. This is a treadmill apparatus that can be set at a predetermined speed according to the capabilities of the dog. Models of these machines have even been modified for Toy dogs. Since the stamina of Toy dogs is much more limited than that of the larger Working Dogs, such equipment would seem to be of limited value. The Toy dog by nature is a bouncy, energetic animal who can usually get sufficient exercise in a medium-sized exercise yard. The occasional lazy dog can be walked on a lead for a couple of periods each day to keep up with a proper regimen of exercise.

The three areas of conditioning, then, are: the maintenance of sound health, the feeding of a balanced diet, and the establishment of a sound program of daily exercise. It is not possible to say that one of these areas is less important than any other, for the neglect of one phase cannot be compensated for by an increase in emphasis of another. The program should be carefully planned in advance so that it will become an established routine to which both dog and owner can become readily adjusted. A show dog must be kept in top condition the year round, or he cannot be expected to compete successfully in the conformation ring. Entering a dog that is not in top condition puts him at a serious disadvantage when he is compared with the other dogs and may cause him to lose to an inferior dog. In addition to establishing a bad show record, it is a needless waste of entry fee money. Dedicated breeders will not put a dog out that is not in the best possible condition for fear of destroying the reputation of their kennel. Most professional handlers will not show a dog that has not been properly conditioned. They do not want such a dog to reflect on their judgment of quality. Showing such a dog to a judge might lead to questions of the handler's ability to evaluate honestly and correctly the true worth of a particular specimen. A handler who makes his living by showing other people's dogs cannot afford to build a reputation that he shows poor quality dogs or that he is incapable of evaluating dogs.

It can be concluded, then, that conditioning is of prime importance in showing dogs. It is the one factor that can be modified by the owner or handler to the advantage of the dog. Since nothing can be done to modify the genetic make-up of the dog or his physical structure, the one variable must then receive the greatest attention of the exhibitor.

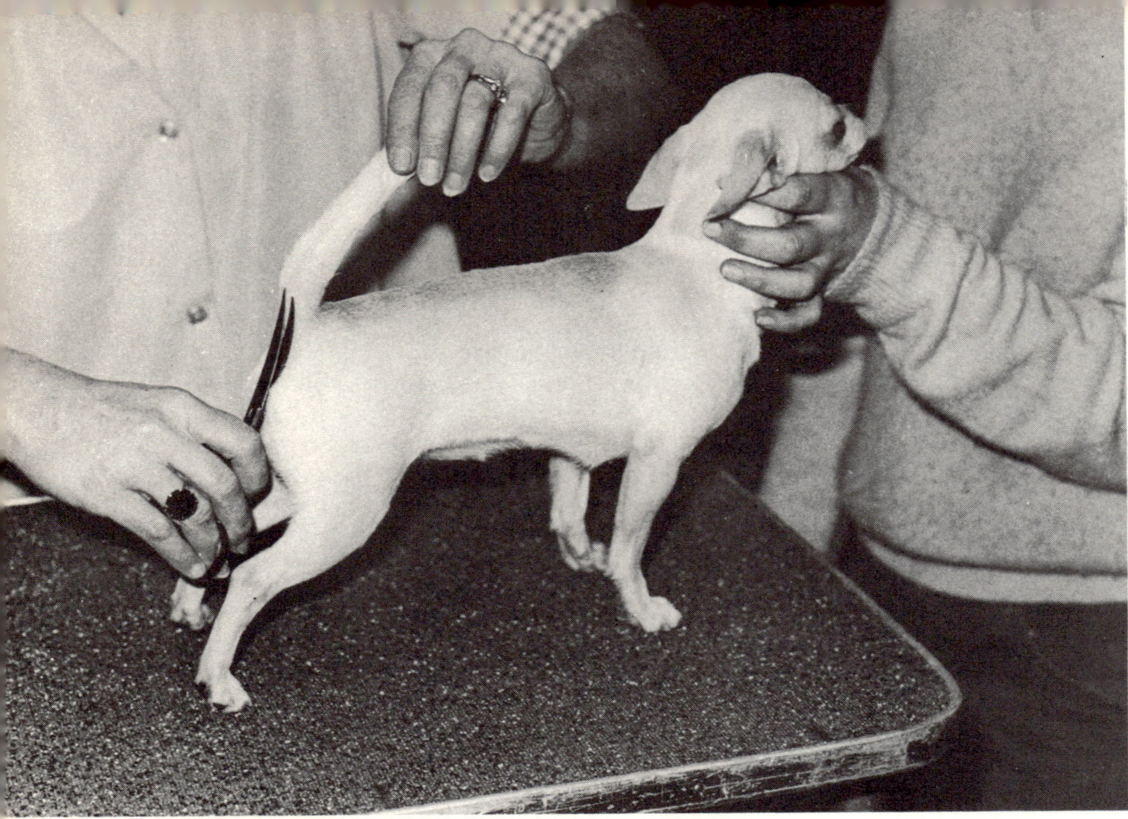

Long hair is trimmed from the rear of the dog.

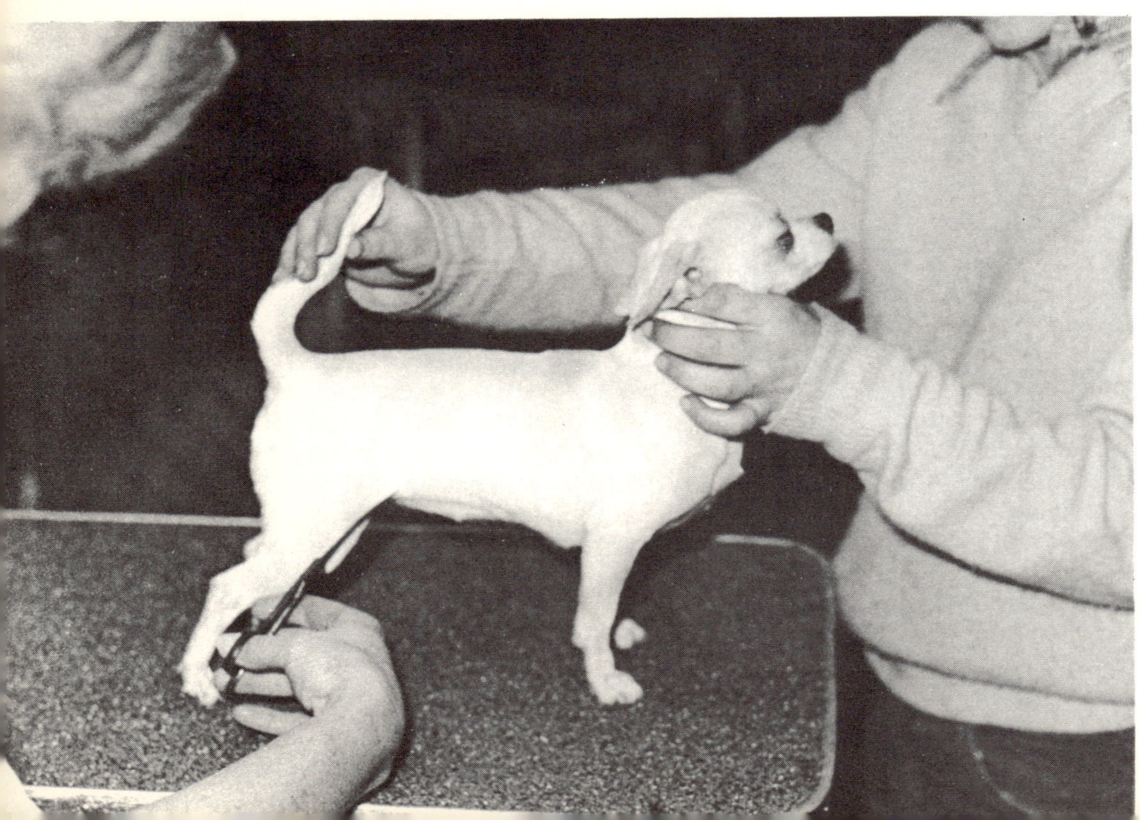

The tuck-up under line is trimmed to remove long hairs.

Before a dog can be groomed properly, he must have been conditioned properly. His general state of health must be good, and his muscles must have been thoroughly toned so that he can be shown to advantage. These qualities depend on diet, exercise, and preventive health care, already discussed in Chapter I, which deals with the conditioning of the dog. A dog in good condition is a pleasure to groom, while one that is underweight, out of coat, or not physically in his prime is difficult to groom and makes grooming an unrewarding chore. The latter can never be groomed to advantage because there is just not enough raw material present to produce a quality specimen.

Training

Before a dog can really be groomed properly so that he can be shown to advantage, he must be lead broken. He, of course, must be lead broken before he can be shown, but this must also be done before he is initially groomed, for that is when he is analyzed as to his physical strengths and weaknesses and the pattern for his grooming established. Every dog has both strong and weak points. The groomer is able to compensate for some of the less strong qualities of the dog by modifying the grooming techniques he will use on an individual dog. For example, in the case of a dog with a hair part on the head, the groomer can change the apparent proportion of the head and modify the expression by adjusting the eye to eye part either up or down. This will cause the muzzle to look either longer or shorter in proportion to the skull and can, therefore, change the apparent balance of the head.

In another situation the groomer can thin the shoulder hair slightly to modify the appearance of the dog that is overloaded in the shoulder. Problems of gait can also be modified by altering the quantity of coat either on the outside or the inside of the leg. A dog's gait cannot be analyzed for grooming needs unless he has been properly lead trained in advance. Trying to groom a dog before analyzing all aspects of his bone and muscle structure and his movement is an unwise undertaking on the part of the groomer. Since many judges go by the overall picture a dog presents in the ring and by his balance, the grooming is extremely important.

Chapter 2

General

Grooming

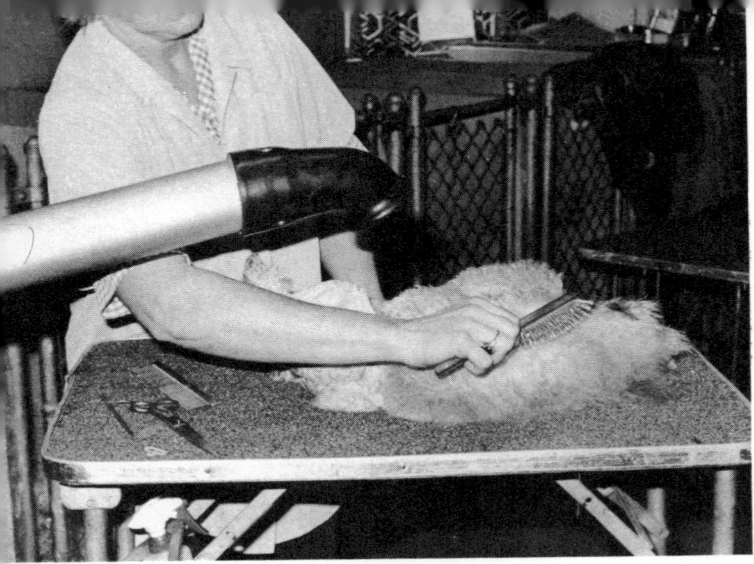

The dog should be trained to
lie on his side for grooming.
An electric dryer will speed
up the drying process.

Training a dog for grooming also means training him to stand in the show pose that he will be required to use when he is in the ring. Specific grooming needs and techniques cannot be adequately designed unless the groomer can analyze the structure of the dog thoroughly. In the case of a high quality dog, no adjustments will have to be made from standard grooming practices, but since many dogs need a little help, individual analysis must be made. If a dog is not properly trained to pose and has a tendency to wiggle or to sit down, the groomer may get a false impression of what will be required to present the dog so that the grooming takes full advantage of all points of quality. When the dog stands calmly, the groomer has an opportunity to examine him in the same manner in which the judge examines him. This enables the groomer to set the basic grooming pattern that will be followed in the future. Occasionally the original pattern will have to be changed either because it was improperly set or because the dog has ma-

The thumb is placed under the
upper lip to force the whiskers
out for trimming.

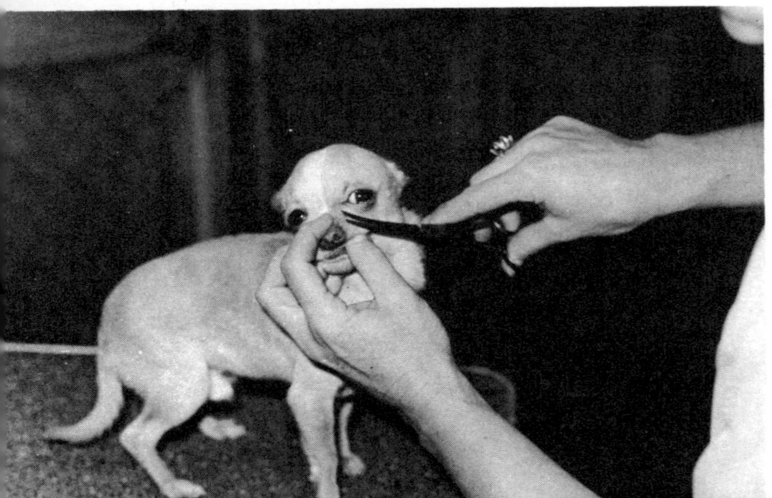

tured and has changed physically from what he was when he was first evaluated. Setting a new grooming pattern in some breeds, such as the Chihuahua, will be no problem, but in other cases, the Poodle for example, months may be required to correct an earlier error. Great care must be used in making the initial evaluation of the dog and in setting the first pattern of grooming.

The third phase of pre-grooming training is that of teaching the dog that he must stand or lie still during grooming sessions. Whether or not this is a problem depends on the individual dog and on the early training he received when he was a puppy. Training to lie down and to stand still for grooming is started when the puppy is still very young—even as early as four or five weeks of age. The puppy's first experience in this area will be the result of his needing to have his nails trimmed. Puppy nails are extremely sharp and grow rapidly. If his nails are not kept short, the puppy may cause injury to the other puppies in the litter. Many early eye injuries are a direct result of nail cuts received when puppies were roughhousing. When a puppy is thrashing and squirming, it is next to impossible to cut his toenails without injuring him. A puppy must be held and gentled and have his feet rubbed daily for some time before he is to have his first nail-cutting session. This will accustom him to the first operation and should make it a less traumatic episode.

Early training includes getting the puppy accustomed to the brush and the comb as well. Socializing young puppies starts long before they are weaned. They are picked up and held and played with so that they will adjust easily to people. The first informal grooming sessions are held during these adjustment periods. It is very easy to brush a puppy gently while holding him on his back in one's lap, and the grooming session can be treated as a game or as a massage at first. When the puppy squirms and turns over, the groomer should continue to groom whatever part of the puppy has been pointed in his direction. It is wise to start with a session of no more than a minute or two the first time. Later sessions can be lengthened and discipline can be added so that by the time the dog has enough coat to groom, he will be willing and able to tolerate a long session.

A long-coated dog must be trained to lie on his side while he is being groomed. This is the only way in which the groomer can get at the underside of the dog. This area must be groomed thoroughly and frequently because there is a tendency for this hair to mat more than the top hair of the dog. When the dog runs and plays the hair becomes entangled and mats can develop easily. It is next to impossible to groom the underside of a Toy dog while he is standing. Grooming the inside of the legs can be done properly only while the dog is lying on his side. The average dog will learn to lie on his side if the trainer has exerted the necessary influence and has been consistent in not allowing the puppy to misbehave while he is being trained. There are a few dogs, however, that almost seem to be untrainable when it comes to teaching them to lie down for grooming. In some cases it takes a matter of months to achieve even a minimal level of cooperation. Sometimes it requires one person to hold and a second person to brush before the dog learns the procedure. In other cases it is possible to hold with one hand and brush with the other. It should be emphasized that the earlier this training is started the easier and more successful it will be.

Pet Grooming

While this book is designed basically for show grooming, a word should be said about grooming the family pet. Very few owners of pet dogs are willing to spend the amount of time grooming their dog that a show coat would require. A dog that runs through the fields and romps with the children would ruin a show coat in a very brief period of time. In the case of the pet dog, the grooming that will be done will not be for the sake of beauty, but rather to keep the dog healthy and comfortable. In the case of the long coat, the dog will probably be kept in a kennel clip. Regular clipping keeps the hair short enough so that it does not build up mats and make the dog uncomfortable. Coats that become excessively matted will break the skin and allow infection to set in. Unbrushed long coats are also an invitation to fleas and ticks during the warm months. Keeping the coat of the pet short will make bathing much easier. It is easier to rinse soap out of a short coat and it is much easier to dry the dog. Grooming for the pet dog, then, is based on comfort and hygiene for the dog and on convenience for the owner.

Show Grooming

Maintaining a show coat on a long-coated Toy dog is not a task to be undertaken by the weak of heart or the weak of back. Grooming full coats requires many hours of work each week and establishes a schedule that must be adhered to on a daily basis. Regularity is one of the most important aspects of show grooming. The fine hair of Toy dogs is delicate and can easily be damaged. Because it is so fine, it mats quickly. The only way to keep matting to a minimum, and thereby prevent a loss of coat, is to brush the dog every day or every other day, depending on the texture of the coat. This frequency is important for the protection of the coat and it also establishes a pattern of training to which the dog can easily become adjusted.

When grooming the Toy dog, great care must be exercised. No matter what piece of equipment is used on the dog, it should be used gently. Rapid or rough grooming will break coat which may have taken months to grow. It will require months more to have it grow back. This is not the only result of breaking coat. Once a hair has been broken, the end becomes rough and tends to dry out owing to the loss of natural oil. In addition to this, the rough end will rub against the remaining long hair, damaging the hair sheath. This weakened hair will become brittle and will break, further complicating the maintenance of a show coat. Professional groomers have learned to avoid these difficulties and can even correct some situations that their clients have caused while trying to keep up the show coat at home. The handlers' years of experience come into play in saving and protecting coat. But coats at times pass even beyond that which a handler can correct.

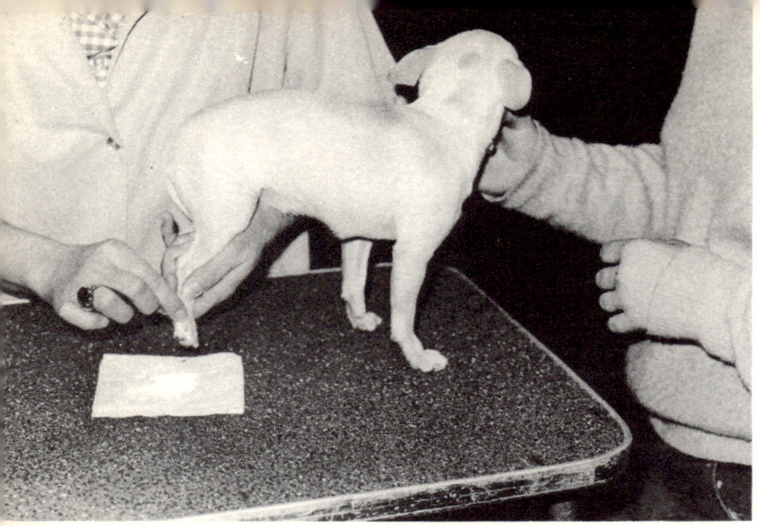

The dog's feet may be chalked
to remove dirt and oil.

When the amateur discovers that he has started the coat on a downhill plunge toward ruin, he really has a problem. One reason for this is that things are usually much worse than the novice realizes and it may already be too late for easy correction. Frequently, even when the condition is detected, the amateur does not have the know-how to amend it.

To avoid these problems, grooming sessions should be started while the puppy is very young and before he has much coat. This will enable the owner to learn on a short, easily maintained coat. It can be hoped that the groomer will learn good grooming techniques by the time the coat is mature. The coat grows much faster the first year than it does in any other single year of the dog's life, so this coat must be protected as carefully as the mature coat.

The grooming of specific coats will be dealt with in later chapters covering the individual breeds, but it is possible to make some generalizations here regarding the use of the brushes

A dampened cloth is used to
clean the area under the eye.

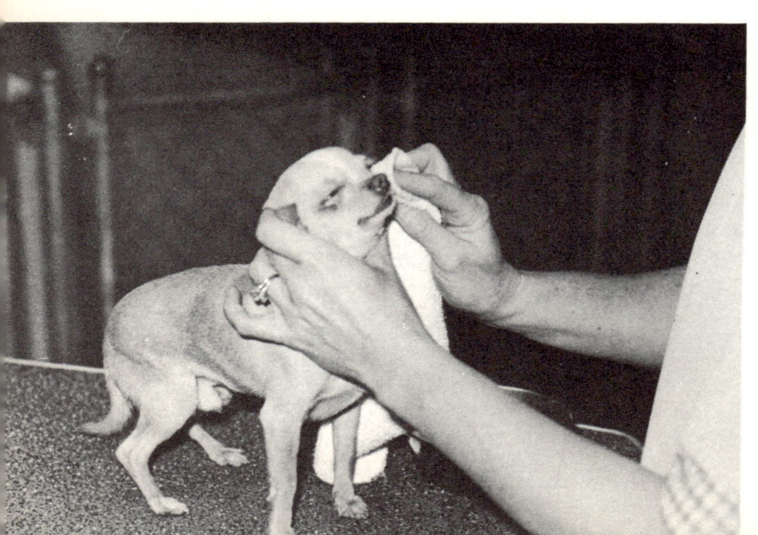

and combs that will be required in the grooming of all dogs.

Whatever tool is being used should be used gently. The brushing or combing motions must be slow, easy, and steady. They should be performed with the hand and forearm moving as a single unit and not with wrist action alone. Wrist action is too vigorous, for the final follow-through motion is at a much higher rate of speed than the initial motion. It can be compared with the children's game of cracking the whip on ice skates. The last member of the line has to move much more rapidly while turning than the rest of the skaters, and as a result control is lost. The arm moves through a similar though more gentle arc while grooming, and losing control of brush or comb action at this time will break coat.

By using gentle, long strokes it is easy to detect snags or mats or foreign objects that have become caught in the coat. Any pulling on a comb or brush means that the action should be stopped immediately and the difficulty analyzed. Twigs and grass can be pulled out with the fingers, and snags and small mats can also be worked out with the fingers or the single tooth of a comb. If the hair sticks together because of mud or dirt, it should be sprayed with water before being brushed. If the dog is really dirty, he should be bathed before being groomed in order to save as much coat as possible. It would be a rare occasion for a show dog in full coat ever to be in this condition, for he should just never be put into a situation where this can occur. Thorough grooming must penetrate down to the skin, and then the coat must be groomed from the skin out to eliminate all skin mats. A dog that is properly groomed on a regular basis will not develop these small mats.

Line-brushing, or layer-brushing, is one of the grooming techniques that is used on the medium-coated and long-coated dogs. With the dog lying on its side, the groomer starts brushing the hair on the stomach, moving from right to left. When he reaches the end of this row of brushing, the groomer starts over again, moving the part-line up an inch or two, and continues in this fashion up the side of the dog until he reaches the part down the spine. He then turns the dog over and repeats the process. This technique guarantees that the entire coat has been brushed thoroughly. Correct brushing techniques, a regular schedule for grooming, and keeping the dog's coat clean are the three keys to success in maintaining a beautiful show coat.

Bathing is an important ritual for show dogs that are being kept in full coats. It is part of the weekly routine for dogs being campaigned, and may even, in the case of long-coated dogs, be a weekly exercise while at home in the kennel growing coat. Before bathing the dog, however, there are things that should be checked: the nails, the teeth, and the ears.

Nails

Toenails should be cut regularly, starting when the puppy is very young—even before he is weaned. Cutting the nails on the young puppy will train him to the procedure and he will, therefore, not resent the treatment when he is an adult.

The nails should be kept trimmed back so that they do not touch the ground when the dog is standing. Care will have to be exercised so that the nail is not trimmed back so far that the vein will be cut—which not only is painful to the dog but also will cause bleeding. The vein in the white nail can be seen easily, but not the vein in the black nail. It is better to make several small cuts than one larger one that might damage the vein. Cutting the vein is not a serious problem, but it should be avoided if at all possible. In some cases a dog's nails may already have reached an unacceptable length before the groomer has an opportunity to trim them. In this case it may be necessary to take the dog to the veterinarian and have him put under a general anesthetic. While the dog is under anesthesia, the veterinarian will cut the nails back to the length they should be and will then have to cauterize the bleeding veins. The dog will have sore toes for a day or two but will suffer no long-range discomfort. This operation is kinder to the dog than allowing him to walk on excessively long nails. The long nails produce back-pressure on the toes with every step and will eventually cause the toes to spread, twisting the nails and resulting in a splayed foot.

The nails can be cut by the groomer with any of a number of special cutters designed for this purpose, or they can be filed. A supply of styptic powder should be kept on hand to stop any bleeding in case the nail is cut too deeply. In

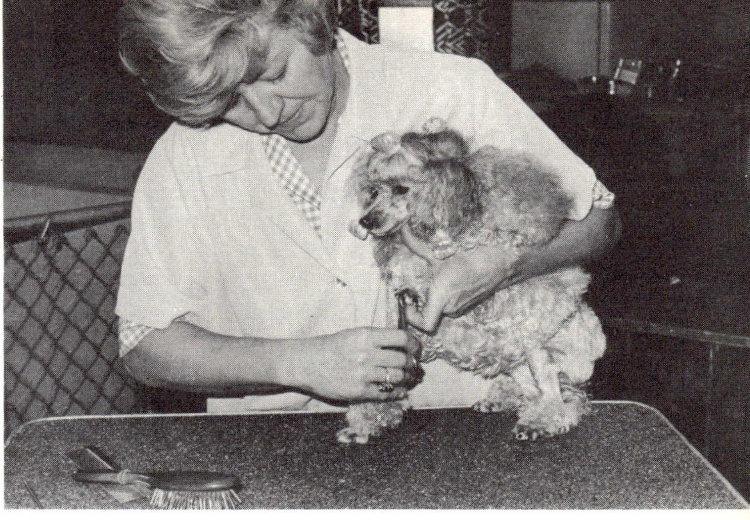

Nails should be trimmed once a week. They may be cut, filed, or ground with an electric grinder.

addition to the guillotine cutters, special little motor-driven electric grinders are also available. These are very efficient and do not cause bleeding. Some dogs seem to be made nervous by the sound of the motor the first time or two, but most adjust easily.

Teeth

At the same time that the dog's nails are trimmed, his teeth should be checked to make sure that there is no accumulation of tartar. The dog should be allowed to chew on hard biscuits or bones to keep the teeth scraped clean of tartar. If this is not accomplished by chewing, the teeth will have to be scraped with a dental pick. It is important to keep tartar off the teeth, for an accumulation will cause the teeth to decay and they will have to be removed earlier than would otherwise be necessary.

The teeth should be scraped every two to three weeks with a dental pick.

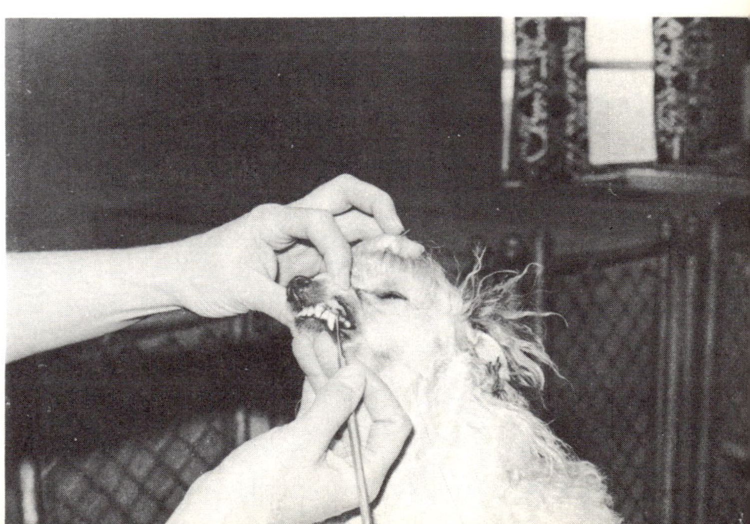

The puppy's first set of teeth come in when he is between six and eight weeks of age. The mature set of teeth comes in between six and eight months of age. Occasionally in Toy dogs some of the baby teeth will not come out by themselves. In this case they will have to be pulled to make room for the adult teeth and to allow them to come in straight. In the excessively small dogs it is not at all uncommon to find a double row of adult teeth. One row will obviously have to be removed. It would be wise, in the long run, to eliminate from a breeding program those dogs which produce double rows of teeth.

Ears

A number of breeds of Toy dogs have pendant ears, or ears which hang down, completely covering the ear opening. Because the ear leather tends to stop the circulation of air and helps to retain moisture, ear infections frequently develop. Hair, therefore, should be pulled from the ear and wax should regularly be removed. To clean the ear thoroughly, one should dip a cotton ball in a little alcohol and, wringing it out completely, use it as a swab.

During the summer months the dog may be bothered by ear mites. There are a number of commercial medicines available that are effective in treating this condition.

To keep the hair pulled out of the ears, the fingers can be used where the ear opening is large. When the ear is small, it is more efficient to use a pair of tweezers or a hemostat. When these metal instruments are used, the dog will

have to lie perfectly still. Should he wiggle or move, the instrument might damage the ear. To counteract any irritation that might occur, it is wise to swab the ear with a medicated ear ointment following the removal of the hair.

When bathing the dog, care must be exercised to prevent water from getting into the ear. One procedure to eliminate this problem is to put a cotton ball loosely into the ear cavity before bathing the dog. The cotton will serve as a plug to prevent water from entering and will thus prevent any excessive irritation to the ear.

Bathing

Bathing does not hurt the dog's coat or affect his health providing it is done with care. Show dogs are usually bathed once a week, and they are still able to grow beautiful coats. It is wise, however, to avoid needless bathing, and every effort should be made to keep the dog clean in order to avoid this possibility. A clean exercise yard helps keep the dog clean and precludes unnecessary bathing.

Before a dog is bathed he should be brushed to ascertain that his coat does not have any mats. Bathing a mat only tends to make it more difficult to work out. Brushing a short-coated dog before bathing will eliminate some of the dry, soft dirt and most of the dandruff. Brushing a long-coated dog whose hair has been up in wraps will help to keep the hair straight during the soaping process. In the case of a dog whose coat is sticky or caked with mud, it is wisest to bathe him first and brush him later. This will prevent breaking the hair ends.

Before bathing the dog, the owner should put a little medicated ointment in each eye. This will protect the eye against irritation should some of the soapy water get into it. The eye should be protected in all breeds, but it is especially important in those breeds which have the large prominent eye, such as the Pekingese and the Shih Tzu.

The best arrangement for bathing a dog is to stand him in a tub with high sides and use a hose with a spray nozzle so that the flow of water can be directed to any particular spot. In no case should the tub be filled to allow the dog to stand in water. A rubber mat in the bottom of the tub will give the dog a feeling of security and prevent his slipping, which could cause a sprain. Some dogs get overly active when they have the

Ointment should be put into the dog's eyes to protect them from soap during the bath.

confidence of a mat under them. Their security will disappear and their self-discipline will return if the mat is removed. They will be forced to stop wiggling in order to avoid falling.

First the dog should be thoroughly wet down with warm water. Then a solution of soap should be poured over him and worked into a lather. In the case of long-coated dogs, the soap is not rubbed to form a lather, but rather patted into the coat. Rubbing long hair will cause it to become entangled, which could cause damage to the hair shaft. The hair is in its weakest state when it is wet, so unnecessary agitation should be avoided.

Commercial pet supply companies have a number of soap products designed specifically for dogs. There are even special soaps for special coats, and soaps have been designed for Poodles to enhance the various colors of coats. Veterinarians can also supply good soap products, including those with medication added to relieve skin irritation or kill fleas and ticks. Commercial products should be used with caution the first few times in order to determine the reaction of a particular dog. Occasionally a dog appears sensitive to a shampoo or rinse. In this case, the dog should be bathed again with a medicated shampoo to offset the reaction. If a rash develops, a veterinarian should be consulted.

In the case of a dog that has been down in oil, a second or even third soaping may be necessary to remove all traces of the oil. After soaping, the dog must be rinsed thoroughly. The rinsing is certainly as important as the soaping, and may be even more important. Soap residue left in the hair will dull it and may even burn the coat. The rinsing process will always take more time than the soaping.

It is wise to use a creme rinse on the coat after rinsing thoroughly with plain water. A commercial product made especially for dogs is best. It may be left on the coat for as long as five minutes and then rinsed out. This is an important step in the case of long-haired dogs, for it will keep down matting and help to eliminate static electricity.

Excess water should be squeezed from the coat after the last rinse and the dog should be wrapped in towels for several minutes to help absorb even more of the water. To speed up the drying process and to eliminate wave or curl in the coat, an electric dryer should be used. It should never be used in the high heat position,

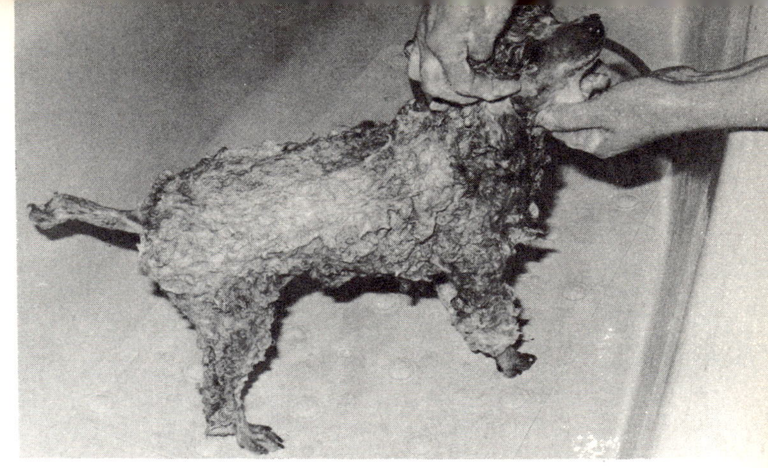

The soap should be rubbed or patted thoroughly into the coat. A second sudsing may be necessary if the dog has been down in oil.

however, because of the danger of scorching the coat. With the warm air blowing on the dog, the coat should be brushed out gently with the pin brush. This will separate each hair and allow it to dry individually, thus eliminating any tendency to wave. After brushing the dog completely dry, the groomer should repeat the process, brushing the hair in small layers and checking each layer with a comb to be certain that there are no small mats left.

Caution must be exercised when using the large commercial hair dryers—not only with the heat setting, but also with the air-flow speed. If the air speed is set too high, the hair will dry in sections before it can be brushed properly and separated. This will cause the hair to be a little stiff and allow it to curl even after it has been separated. It would be almost like a mild permanent wave, for the hair would be dried in a pattern and that pattern would be set. Large commercial dryers are expensive, but they can save hours of drying time during a show season. They also shorten the length of time during which the dog must be kept immobile while being dried—which will certainly add to his comfort and contentment.

The first day or two after a bath the coat must receive special attention, for all of the natural oil will have been removed and the hair will be dry. Dry hair is brittle and will build up charges of static electricity which will cause it to mat. As a result, the dog will have to be brushed daily with great care to prevent any damage to the coat.

The quantity and texture of coat of the Toy dogs vary considerably. Special attention and techniques are mentioned in the specific chapters dealing with the various breeds.

Best-in-Show Ch. Hurd's Honey Bee, Smooth Coat Chihuahua, owned by Max Hurd and Teddye Dearborn.

Ch. Paradise Conquistador, Long Coat Chihuahua, owned by Ann Stockton.

Chapter 3

Short-Coated Toy Dogs

The short-coated Toy dogs such as the Chihuahua, the Italian Greyhound, the Toy Manchester, the Miniature Pinscher, and the Pug require the least amount of grooming. Dogs of diminutive size and with short coats will not require the hours of grooming that either the long-coated dogs or the larger dogs will require. The fact that they do not demand great amounts of time for grooming does not mean that their grooming should be neglected. Even the short-coated Toy requires pre-ring grooming in order to look his best.

The objective of grooming the short coat is to make the dog look as neat as possible. His coat should be clean and should have been brushed with a polishing technique so that it has the gloss or sheen which is identified with a healthy coat. Short-coated dogs do shed with the change of seasons, so there will be times when even this small amount of coat will not be in prime condition. Conscientious grooming on a regular basis will help minimize the problem, however.

The dog's nails should be trimmed every week, but they should receive special attention a day or two before the show. Cutting the nails this far in advance will allow healing time should one of the nails be cut too deeply. The nails should be kept trimmed back so far that they do not touch the ground. Nails that strike the ground will force the toes to spread and will prevent the dog from standing well up on his feet.

Smooth-coated dogs should have their whiskers trimmed. This can be done the day of the show, for if it is done any earlier, the whiskers will grow back and will have to be trimmed again. This can be a frustrating exercise, for the dogs seem to be able to pull the whiskers in while they are being trimmed. One technique is to slip a finger into the dog's mouth and under the lip, and force the whiskers to extend as far as possible. They can then be trimmed back with a blunt-nosed scissors. Not only are the upper lip and chin whiskers trimmed but also the eyebrows and any other long stiff hairs that grow on the face, chin, or neck areas. This will give a much cleaner appearance to the head.

The eyes of many dogs tend to tear. In some breeds tearing occurs because the eye is too large, while in other breeds it occurs because the eye is too small. This constant moisture at the inner corner of the eye causes eye stain—the result of the moisture's mixing with dirt which will eventually produce a brown or reddish stain. While many dogs have the eye stain problem, it is particularly obvious in the white dog. Daily attention can keep the condition to an acceptable minimum. When the condition becomes exaggerated, it can be treated with a mild solution of boric acid or fuller's earth mixed into a paste and rubbed into the stained hair, making certain that none of it gets into the eye.

This latter treatment is not for the day of the show. At the show the stained area is cleaned with a dampened cloth. While this will not correct a condition of long standing, it will remove any dirt accumulated since the bath the day before. A small amount of talcum powder or chalk can be rubbed into the area and allowed to dry. When thoroughly dry it should be brushed out. This will help to remove any excess skin oil that might be complicating the situation.

The dog's ears should be cleaned to make certain that they are free from all traces of wax. A cotton swab moistened with alcohol will remove wax and allow the ear to dry rapidly.

These are the general grooming practices that will be required for all Toy dogs with short coats in getting them ready for the ring. The five short-coated breeds will be discussed individually in the remainder of this chapter so that problems peculiar to each individual breed can be accentuated.

Chihuahua—Smooth Coat

Special attention is always given to the analysis of the head of the Chihuahua. Breeders are especially concerned that they breed for the correct proportion of eye, ear, and skull. The shape of the head is particularly important. The smoothness of the grooming of the head can enhance the natural traits of the dog, so the head hair must be groomed smoothly so that it lies flat and close to the head. An unruly hair here or there will destroy the smoothness and should be clipped off.

Eye stain is occasionally a problem with the Chihuahua. While this condition should receive attention daily, it should receive special attention the day of the show. As much of the stain

as possible should be removed either with a damp cloth or with chalk. Excessive eye stain could tend to indicate to the judge that there may be an eye problem, so the less obvious the stain can be made, the better picture the dog will present.

The edges of the ears should be trimmed of any uneven hair. This does not mean that there is to be a general trimming of the ear, but rather an evening up so that the delicate outline of the ear is not affected. In the case where there is an excessive amount of hair growing in the ear itself, the hair should be trimmed to blend in a smooth flowing line with the line of the skull. This is a matter of hygiene as much as a cosmetic treatment.

The neck and shoulder line of the dog should be groomed into a smooth flowing line. If a smooth-coated Chihuahua has an exceptionally heavy coat and is in very good weight, there may be a bunching up of hair where the neck coat joins the shoulder coat. The thickness here and the length of the hair itself may give the impression that the neck or shoulder is out of proportion when this is really not the case. To help correct this situation and make the true outline obvious, the handler may wish to use a pair of thinning shears so that the real body line can be seen. The shears are held parallel to the back, pointed in the direction opposite that in which the hair grows. One or two cuts over each shoulder or where the bunching up occurs should suffice to smooth out the neck line. A stripping comb may be used instead of the thinning shears. No such thinning should be attempted if the dog is the least bit low in shoulders, for this will only exaggerate the condition.

The top line of the back should be smoothed thoroughly. If there is any dead or loose hair standing up, it should be removed. From the top down around the sides of the dog, the coat should present a smooth, uninterrupted line.

The under line of the dog may require a little evening up, for this is an area where the hair does not all grow in the same direction. The hair on the thin skin that joins the rear leg to the side of the dog will require a little trimming to make the hair line conform to the skin line under it. This is best done with a blunt-nosed, curved scissors. Trimming under the dog may be necessary if the hair stands out around the breasts, for the under line should be as smooth and uninterrupted as the top line.

The hindquarters of the Chihuahua may also require a little trimming, especially where the hair line of the side coat meets the hair line of the rump. This usually results in a ridge which continues part way down the rear legs. In the case of the heavier coated dog, the line may be too prominent and thick and should be trimmed back to give a more even appearance. The tail of the Chihuahua should be trimmed of any straggly hair.

The feet should be trimmed so that the hair line is even and barely covers the nails. Excessive hair should be trimmed from between the pads of the feet so that the dog can get good traction when gaiting.

The amount of trimming required on a smooth-coated Chihuahua will depend on the texture and quantity of the coat, and the less grooming required, the better the coat. A smooth-coated Chihuahua should not have an excessively heavy coat that would require a great deal of trimming. It would be wise not to include a dog with an excessively heavy coat in a breeding program.

Chihuahua—Long Coat

The grooming concerns of the long-coated Chihuahua are really quite different from those of the smooth-coated variety. With the long coat, the exhibitor will want to keep as much hair as possible. The whiskers will be trimmed, but that may be all that is required in the way of trimming.

The eyes should be cleaned, and the ears should be kept free of wax. Excessive hair should be trimmed from between the pads of the feet to give the dog full advantage of good traction when gaiting.

In grooming the body coat, the hair should be brushed carefully in the direction in which it grows. Grooming may require the use of an oil coat dressing to prevent breaking hair ends while brushing. Ear fringes and tail hair should be brushed carefully to avoid unnecessary loss of coat. Since the coat is the essential difference between the two varieties of Chihuahua, the coat should be well cared for in order to underscore this important distinction.

Feathering on the legs is especially important for the long-coated Chihuahua. Because it is one of his distinctive traits, care must be exercised to protect the feathering. The foot hair may have to be rinsed with a high degree of regularity to keep it free from dirt, which tends to make the hair brittle and allows it to break. Rinsing with warm water should suffice. Keeping this hair in a light oil will give additional protection. The hair should be brushed so that it will lie flat against the body, especially on the chest and the rump. This will shorten the apparent body length of the dog.

Italian Greyhound

The Italian Greyhound is a Coursing Hound in miniature. Even standing still he should give the impression of grace and motion. He must have a streamlined appearance, allowing nothing to interrupt the flowing outline of his body. Because the coat is so smooth and fine, the least rumple of hair will look like a major fault.

The whiskers of the upper lips are trimmed off, as are those of the chin. Eyebrows are trimmed and so are any other long hairs that occasionally appear on the head. Slipping the finger under the upper lip will force the whiskers out so that they can be trimmed as short as possible. It is not really necessary to trim the whiskers at home, but it is essential to do this the day of the show.

Tearing will cause the reddish-brown stain under the eyes that detracts from the typical expression of the Italian Greyhound. The area under the eyes should be cleaned carefully to remove any evidence of tearing. If the problem is severe, a solution of boric acid or fuller's earth can be used at home. It should not be used the day of the show, however. If staining is of little significance, talcum powder or chalk may be rubbed under the eye to pull out any accumulation of oil which will cause a blemish. It is important that there be no discoloration in the eye area, for a discolored area may give the impression that the eye is slightly different in size or shape than it actually is. Dark stain will give the impression that the eye is larger than it should be, and, by comparison, the dark stain will cause the eye to look light when it may not be. Keeping the area free from unnatural coloration will help keep the dog looking his best.

Trimming around the ear may be required occasionally. The hair covering the ear is so fine and smooth that this will usually not be the case. However, if the hair at the edges looks a little uneven, it can be trimmed smooth.

Only seldom does an Italian Greyhound require any scissor work. This would only be needed when a hair or two has been damaged and tends to stand out rather than lie flat. This occurs more frequently in the young dog than in the older one. Snipping off such stray hairs will restore the natural outline. The dog can be sprayed all over and then rubbed dry with a towel to get the hair to lie in the right direction. When toweling the dog, the groomer should be careful to use strokes going in the same direction in which the hair grows. This is not a back and forth action, but rather only one from front to back, which will prevent bending the hair and will force it to lie flat and follow the body line.

The under line of the dog may need a little trimming to achieve a continuous, uninterrupted, flowing line. This is especially true in the breast area where any slight swelling can result in a disproportionate protrusion of hair. The thin skin line where the hind leg joins the side of the body may need a slight trimming to give a clear view of the tuck-up. Any hairs that are longer than the rest should be cut back so that they are all of the same length.

Hindquarters again will need little work. However, it may be necessary at times to trim a straggly hair here or there to achieve the smooth outline. On the rear of the dog the hair changes growth direction where side hair and back hair meet. If a slight ridge results from this growth pattern, the ridge should be trimmed down so that it does not look exaggerated.

The feet should be trimmed of any hair that extends lower than the pad line of the toe. The hair should be cut so that it does not cover the base of the toenails. Hair should also be trimmed out from between the toes. This will give the dog better traction and help to keep the toes held tightly together. Hair growing between the pads of the feet will cause the toes to spread and make the foot look disproportionately large for the dog.

The hair on the tip of the tail may need to be evened a little. Since hair does not grow at an even rate over the entire body, cosmetic trimming will help to offset any slight irregularity. It is really surprising how a few hairs out of place will assume exaggerated proportions on a dog as small as the Italian Greyhound.

When all trimming has been finished, the dog should be sprayed lightly with coat dressing and then toweled dry, rubbing only in the direction in which the hair grows. This will pull all the hair in the same direction and bring out the natural luster of the coat. The satin-like texture of the coat is of great importance in the Italian Greyhound and this final treatment will enhance the general appearance of the coat.

Toy Manchester

The Toy Manchester is groomed to give him a slick, smooth appearance. Very little work will be required on this trim dog to accomplish the desired effect. Trimming will be limited to removing the irregular hairs that might have a tendency to stand out and disrupt the outline.

Whiskers and isolated long hairs on the head will be trimmed as short as possible. The lip whiskers can be forced out to the best position for clipping by slipping the finger under the upper lip and applying a slight pressure from within. The long hairs under the muzzle and on the front of the neck should also be removed.

While eye stain is not a problem in a black coated dog, attention must be given to the eye area to prevent irritation. Just as in the lighter colored dogs, the area should be cleaned thoroughly with a damp cloth to remove any accumulation of foreign matter.

The sloping neck line and the top line should be smoothed down with coat dressing and rubbed dry with a towel, rubbing only in the direction the coat lies naturally, of course. Any hairs that stand up after the coat has dried should be trimmed off so that they do not interrupt the flow of the top line. The same treatment should be applied to the underside of the dog. Hair around the breast area may need to be trimmed a little, as will uneven hair on the underside of the flank skin. Using a pair of curved, blunt scissors will facilitate work in this area and will also ensure that the dog will not be nicked with the sharp point of a regular trimming scissors.

An occasional hair that stands out on the back of the tail or on its tip may also need to be clipped. If a ridge is formed where the side hair and the back hair meet on the rump, the groomer can smooth this down by trimming the point of the ridge.

The feet should be trimmed so that no hair extends beyond the skin line of the pad. The hair above the nails should be cut back even with the root line of the nail. Any hair that grows between the pads of the feet should be trimmed out so that there is no pressure to spread the pads, which could result in a flattened foot.

After the dog has been trimmed, he should be sprayed with a light coat dressing and toweled dry. The toweling should always be done in the direction in which the hair grows. It should never be done with a back and forth motion, for this will rumple the coat excessively. The final touch is to apply a little petroleum jelly to the nails to make them shine.

Miniature Pinscher

The Miniature Pinscher is to be a copy of his giant cousin. He is to give the same appearance of sleekness and power in a very small package. To present this image, his coat must be so groomed that the musculature can easily be seen as the dog stands and gaits. Excessive coat would not permit such an appearance and would be to the serious disadvantage of the dog.

As with the other short-coated dogs, the head whiskers must be cut off. With the finger under the upper lip, the groomer can force the whiskers into the best position for trimming them as short as possible. Eyebrows and other long head and neck hairs should also be cut off at the base. The hair on the edges of the ears should be trimmed so that the outline is as smooth and even as possible.

The dog should be sprayed with a coat dressing and rubbed dry with a towel so that the hair will all lie in the natural direction. To avoid damaging the coat, the towel should be rubbed only in the same direction in which the hair grows. Once the coat is dry, any trimming that should be undertaken can be done. The occasional hair that tends to follow its own direction of growth should be removed so that the outline

of the dog is not broken. This is true not only of the top line, but also of the under line of the dog. Extraneous hairs should be trimmed even with the rest. Special attention must be given to the areas of the breasts where hair will sometimes stand out.

The front of the dog should be examined to see that there are no ridges where the direction of hair growth changes. The bottom of the brisket should be smoothed so that, when viewed from the front, it will present the same even line that it does from the side.

If the coat is the least bit thick or long, ridges will be formed on the rear of the dog where the side hair and rump hair meet. With the scissors held parallel to the skin, the peak of the ridge can be removed, allowing the remaining hair to lie flat against the body. The base of the tail should be smoothed and trimmed if necessary. A little trimming may also be necessary in the curved area between the two back legs.

The feet should be trimmed so that no hair extends beyond the skin line of the pads. The hair should also be trimmed even with the root of the nail, and any hair between the pads of the feet should be removed. With his swift, animated gait, the Miniature Pinscher should have the maximum amount of traction, and by removing this unnecessary hair he will have it. After the hair has been trimmed away from the nails, a little petroleum jelly rubbed on the nails will bring out a shine.

The finishing touches for the Miniature Pinscher before taking him to the ring are to spray him with coat dressing and towel him dry again. Rubbing the coat with a horsehair glove brings a sheen to the coat which highlights the muscled areas of the shoulders and thighs.

Pug

While the Pug is a short-haired dog, his coat is neither so thin nor so short as the other short-haired dogs. The quantity of hair that he carries will require a little more work with the scissors to even out an occasional rough spot.

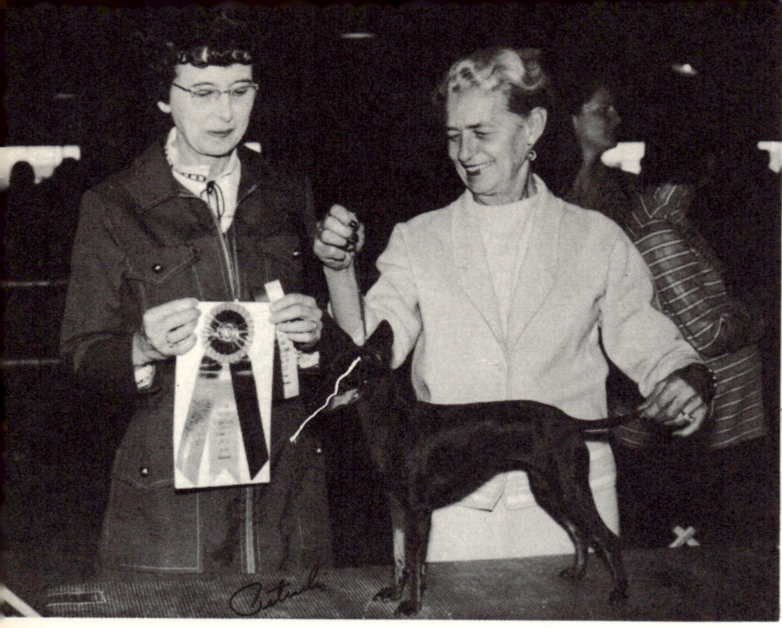

Ch. Blue Chip Sissy Sue, Toy Manchester, owned by Ray E. Messenger.

Head and chin whiskers must be trimmed as short as possible. The thicker lips of the Pug make cutting the whiskers a little more of a task, but with the finger held under the upper lip, whiskers can be forced out to facilitate the cutting. More than some of the other breeds described in this chapter, the Pug has a tendency to produce a few isolated long head hairs. These should all be cut off as close to the skin as possible.

While the Pug's ears should not be trimmed to present the smooth outline that is necessary for the Miniature Pinscher, the occasional long stray hair should be made the same length as the others. It will be necessary to pay special attention to the inside of the ear of the Pug. Because of the folds of the ear or because of the inner part of the ear's being partially covered,

accumulations of wax will build up more rapidly. Ears should be cleaned with a cotton swab moistened with alcohol. This should prevent any infection and keep down irritation.

The large, prominent eyes will have a tendency to tear a little more than smaller eyes. The moistened area under the eye that results from this condition should be cleaned and dried thoroughly to prevent staining. The staining problem is of no consequence in the black dog, but for reasons of hygiene the cleaning should be just as frequent.

The folds on the head can present a problem of irritation if they are especially deep. Irritation is more likely to be a problem in the summer, and certain irritants can complicate the situation. It is especially important to rinse all soap from these areas, for soap curd will cause a

Best-in-Show Ch. Padre Elite Joh-Cyn, Italian Greyhound, owned by the Reverend Robert E. Watson.

Best-in-Show Ch. Allen's Brandy Snifter, Miniature Pinscher, owned by Dr. A. W. Krause.

rash if not completely removed. An occasional treatment with diluted hydrogen peroxide will help alleviate the problem.

When grooming the Pug's body, the groomer should slick down the hair with coat dressing and then towel it dry. Rubbing in the direction of the hair growth with a bristle grooming glove should smooth the coat and make it lie flat. The isolated hair that refuses to lie flat should be cut out. This same principle is followed on both the top line and the under line of the dog.

The ridge of hair formed down the middle of the back legs should be trimmed so that there is no crest and so that the hair will lie flat. The hair in this area does not always grow at the same rate nor from the same direction and will need a little extra attention.

The feet should be trimmed so that the hair does not extend over the pads nor over the nails. Any hair in between the pads should be trimmed away. Special care must be given to the feet and pads of the Pug. Because of his weight, the Pug's feet are under extra stress. The pads should be checked regularly so that no sores are allowed to develop. Regular treatment with hydrogen peroxide eliminates this problem.

Any stray hairs should be trimmed from the tail of the Pug after it has been curled tightly in the way in which the dog will carry it while he is gaiting. The hair on the tip may also be cut to give it an even appearance.

A final treatment with coat dressing and a quick rubdown will be the final grooming touches before the Pug goes into the ring. Rubbing petroleum jelly on each nail and a little on the nose will enhance the natural sheen.

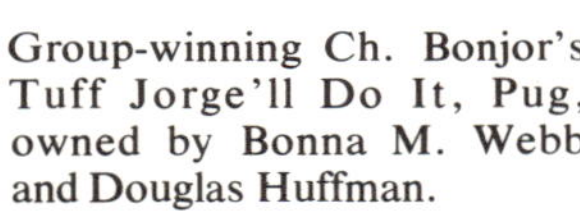

Group-winning Ch. Bonjor's Tuff Jorge'll Do It, Pug, owned by Bonna M. Webb and Douglas Huffman.

Ch. Bluemarc's Hojo leading
the Stud Dog Class at the Na-
tional Specialty of the
Japanese Spaniel Club of
America. This study shows a
variety of poses—some good
and some bad.

Medium-coated Toy dogs such as the English Toy Spaniel, the Japanese Spaniel, the Papillon, the Pomeranian, and the Silky Terrier require a planned grooming schedule that will permit daily or almost daily grooming of the dog. These delicate, fine coats require regular attention if they are to be kept in top show-ring condition at all times. The pattern of the grooming schedule may be on an every other day basis or even a weekly basis if the coat has a good texture. If, however, the coat is excessively soft, it will undoubtedly require daily brushings.

Dogs that fall into this medium-coated category are those whose coats are between two inches and four or five inches long. There is more work with these coats than with the short coats, but they will not require the great quantities of time that the floor-length coats will require. Since the medium coat does not drag the floor, a more streamlined grooming method may be adopted.

There are a few trimming problems that these medium-coated breeds have in common, so they will be dealt with at this point. With the exception of the Pomeranian, all should have their whiskers and eyebrows trimmed as short as possible. If allowed to grow, these longer hairs will push the face hair in different directions and may give the impression that the muzzle is broader than it should be, or that the head is not so smooth or so rounded as the Standard requires.

It is essential to keep the ears clean and free from wax. This is more important in the English Toy Spaniel and the Japanese Spaniel because they have pendant ears and the ear leather covers the ear opening and does not permit a good circulation of air. Cleaning the ears is especially important during the damp summer months, for there seems to be a greater tendency toward ear infections then. The ears can best be cleaned with a cotton swab which is moistened lightly with alcohol and then rubbed over the entire inner surface of the ear opening. The swab will enable the groomer to get in between the folds of the ear and to remove all traces of wax.

Tearing is a problem with many of the Toy breeds. This condition, if not treated regularly, will cause stain at the inner corner of the eyes. While this reddish brown stain will not be noticed on a brown dog, it is quite evident on a dog that has white on its face. When this condition is noted in the dog, it should be treated im-

Chapter 4

Medium-Coated Toy Dogs

mediately. The staining problem can be minimized by brushing in a mixture of boric acid and fuller's earth while the hair is damp. When the mixture dries it can be brushed out. Care will have to be exercised so as not to get any of the powder into the eye. After the area is thoroughly cleaned and dry, a small amount of petroleum jelly can be applied to the affected area. This will act as a waterproofing agent, allowing the tears to run off rather than to penetrate into the hair. This procedure is used only at home and not in the show ring.

The above grooming practices can be applied to all medium-coated Toy dogs. Coat care for the individual breeds differs, so each breed will be treated separately in the remainder of this chapter. If a particular dog has a unique coat problem, different techniques may be required to correct it. What may not normally be a grooming method for a particular breed may have to be adopted to correct the natural condition of a specific dog.

English Toy Spaniel

The English Toy Spaniel with its long, silky, soft, wavy coat will require a gentle grooming hand. Harsh treatment could damage this coat and it might take months to grow the coat back to its original length.

In brushing the body coat, the groomer should use the stainless steel pin brush. These large pins set in soft rubber will flex and give way should they come in contact with a mat. The real objective of grooming is, of course, not to allow mats to develop. Sometimes, however, because of excessive amounts of exercise, a mat will develop. When a mat is detected, it should be worked out gently by pulling the mat in different directions with the fingers and then carefully brushing the area. This procedure should be repeated if the mat does not brush out readily. A small amount of coat dressing or a mist of water containing a small amount of creme rinse will protect the hair ends that may be

stuck together and would break if a brush were forced between them when they were dry, for moisture helps eliminate this problem.

When a section of hair has been brushed completely with the pin brush, the groomer should go over the same section with the comb to determine that there are no small skin mats that the brush did not detect. A small natural-bristle brush can also be used effectively on medium-length coats. The natural bristles are softer than the nylon bristles and will give way to the hair. Also, the natural bristles will not break the hair as the nylon bristles do.

Because the feathering on the legs is important to the appearance of the breed, care must be exercised in brushing so that the hair ends are not damaged. If the hair is allowed to become dry or brittle, it will not grow properly and the dog with a poor coat will be out of balance.

The tail should be treated much in the same manner as the leg furnishings. It should be brushed with the pin brush and sprayed lightly with coat dressing. After it has been brushed thoroughly, the tail hair should be straightened by holding the tip of the tail. With the tail stretched in this fashion, it will be possible to comb it without tangling the comb in the body coat. This will help keep tangling to a minimum and will permit the tail hair to hang properly when the dog gaits.

The hair between the pads of the feet should be trimmed so that the dog will not slip when he is moving. Any other trimming on the feet should be done only for neatness and to even up a straggly hair or two. The top of the feet should be covered with hair and the hair around the foot itself should not be trimmed to give it a precise, clear-cut outline. The hair should be brushed to give the foot a rather soft and indistinct outline.

The ear furnishings should be groomed first with the pin brush and then with the comb to make sure that each hair has been separated from the others. This will give a fullness to the coat and help to keep down any excessive curliness. Should the wavy coat develop a tendency to curl, the groomer should spray the area with coat dressing and then blow it dry with an electric hair dryer set on medium. While the hair is being blown dry, the groomer should brush it gently. This will eliminate a great deal of the curliness. It is important to use a dryer after bathing in order to maintain the proper wavy texture to the coat.

Specialty Best-in-Show Ch. Harco's Monte Cristo, English Toy Spaniel, owned by Harvey Cookman.

Group-winning Ch. Bluemarc's Hojo, Japanese Spaniel, owned by Beulah L. Koontz.

Japanese Spaniel

The grooming of the Japanese Spaniel is similar to that of the English Toy Spaniel. The coat is profuse, long, straight, and rather silky. The main difference between the two breeds is that the coat of the Japanese Spaniel is to be straight rather than wavy. The feet are usually well feathered, which means that the hair on the feet will have to receive special attention.

The prominent eye of the Japanese Spaniel will have a tendency to tear. If the eyes are not cleaned daily, the moistened hair under the eye may become stained. Regular attention to this problem will eliminate discoloration.

Since the ears hang down and cover the ear openings, they will require extra care. The inside of the ears should be cleaned at least once a week with a cotton swab moistened with alcohol. During the summer months it may be necessary to remove the wax more often.

The grooming of the body coat of the Japanese Spaniel is done with the stainless steel pin brush. The flexible pins will be effective in detecting mats but will not break the hair. Once a mat has been detected, it should be worked out with the fingers or with the single tooth of a comb. This method will keep to a minimum the amount of hair lost during grooming.

It is easier on the dog and the groomer if the dog is taught to lie on his side during the grooming sessions. The hair can thus be pushed back for layer brushing without allowing it to fall back over the area being brushed.

Special care must be given to the ruff, for the hair in the neck area has a tendency to mat more rapidly than that of the side coat. The constant movement of the head and the ears causes the hair to tangle.

After the coat has been brushed thoroughly with the pin brush, the groomer covers the same area again with the comb. This separates the individual hairs and smooths the coat, thus giving the dog a sleek appearance.

With the tail held straight out and the hair falling to either side, the groomer should first brush and then comb the hair, separating it carefully. Leg furnishings are groomed in the same fashion as is the hair on the tail. The smooth hair on the legs can be groomed with a slicker brush.

The tufts on the feet enhance the elegant appearance of the Japanese Spaniel. If a dog is allowed to run freely in the yard, he will quickly accumulate dirt and mud in his foot hair. Before grooming the dirty hair, the groomer should either bathe the feet or moisten them so that the ends of the hair will not be broken during the grooming process. Some trimming may be necessary on the feet, especially on the sides and the back, to present a neat picture. There should never be excessive trimming, nor should the trimming round the tufted appearance of the foot into a smooth line. The somewhat casual appearance is the desired one.

After brushing the dog completely, the groomer should spray the coat with a light coat dressing and then brush it dry. The coat may have a slight tendency to wave after a bath. Dampening the coat slightly and blowing it dry with an electric dryer will eliminate this condition. The coat should be brushed continuously during the drying process.

Papillon

Since the silky coat of the Papillon has no undercoat to protect it, extra care must be taken during the grooming session to prevent any needless loss of coat. This is especially true with the ear fringes and the neck frill. The ear fringes in particular must be protected or the dog will not have the "butterfly look" that is required by the Standard.

Before brushing the coat, the groomer should spray it with a light coat dressing. This will protect the hair ends and will loosen daily accumulations of dirt. A pin brush is used for the initial grooming, but once the coat has been brushed completely, it should be combed. The combing is important, for it will remove any tangles that the brush missed, and it will also help keep the coat tangle-free for a longer time.

Ch. Dorken's Tyger Lilly,
American and Canadian C.D.,
Papillon, owned by Beverly
Caliendo.

Ch. Sylvia's Wee Apollo,
Pomeranian, owned by Sylvia
J. Posateri.

The plume on the tail and the feathering on the legs will be treated in the same way as is the frill. Because of the silky nature of the coat, the final combing is important. This separates the hair and allows it to hang straight. An improperly groomed coat does not present the correct picture of a dog whose hair lengths vary on different parts of the body.

While the feet themselves are not trimmed, some scissoring may be needed to make the tufts a little neater. The hair should also be trimmed from between the pads.

The final step in making the Papillon ready for the ring is to spray him with a light mist of coat dressing and brush him dry once more. This will bring out the natural highlights of the coat and give a little added sheen.

Pomeranian

Because the Pomeranian carries a double coat, he will require special grooming techniques. The difference in texture between the undercoat, which is dense and soft, and the outer coat, which is coarse and harsh, makes the special techniques necessary.

Many groomers have difficulty teaching the Pomeranian to lie on his side for grooming sessions. No matter how challenging this task may be, however, it is still worth the effort to teach the dog to lie on his side, for then the grooming will go much more rapidly and easily.

The coat is first sprayed with a mist of coat dressing or a mixture of water and creme rinse. It is then brushed with a small stainless steel pin brush or a natural-bristle brush. The brush will detect any tangles or mats. Tangles should be worked out with the fingers and then brushed gently. Great care must be taken to preserve as much undercoat as possible on the Pomeranian while still eliminating the mats. Gentle but thorough brushing down to the skin is necessary. Neither the slicker brush nor a comb should ever be used on the big coat of the Pomeranian. In getting the dog ready for the ring, the groomer sprays the coat with coat dressing and brushes it in thoroughly with the steel pin brush. The dog is then put in his crate

for approximately thirty minutes so that he may dry completely. He is then brushed very gently again, using a light mist of coat dressing. This procedure will give the solid, cobby body look to the dog.

The tail should be held straight out from the body and all hair should be brushed in the same direction, parallel to the tail and away from the base. When completely brushed, the tail is laid over the back and the hair brushed toward the head, fan-like, from the root of the tail. The tail will have to be replaced and brushed frequently during the showing process in order to keep the hair properly in place. All body hair is also brushed forward toward the head, while the hair on the legs is brushed straight down.

The feet should be trimmed to give them a neat outline, and the hair should be cut out from between the pads. Rubbing the nails and the nose with a little petroleum jelly will enhance the overall appearance of the dog and give a little more contrast to the black.

The points of the ears should be trimmed so that the tiny tips can be seen clearly. Since the ears are important in the judging of the Pomeranian, and the dog must use them to show animation, the accenting of the tips will call attention to their placement and movement. Judicious trimming of the ears is very important, especially if the ear set is not quite correct.

Silky Terrier

The Silky Terrier requires a thorough and careful brushing to make the coat lie flat against his body. With the dog lying on his side, the body coat should be brushed layer by layer from the stomach up to the part, using the stainless steel pin brush or a natural-bristle brush. Any tangles should be removed carefully by pulling out one hair at a time. This will save as much of the coat as is possible. It is easiest to brush under the muzzle and on the neck areas while the dog is lying on his side. This will cause the dog the least amount of discomfort, for he will not have to strain to hold his head high so the groomer can work under the muzzle.

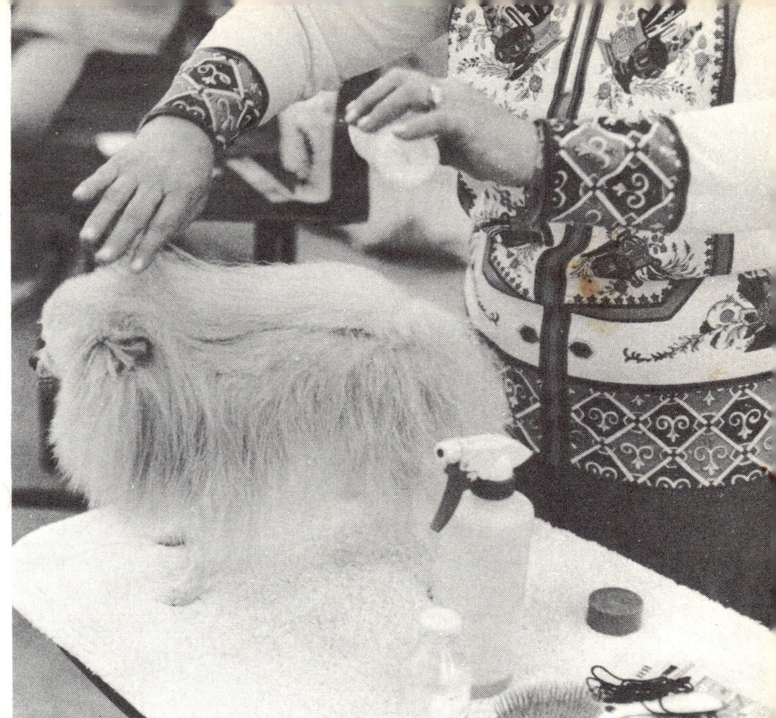

The right side of the dog should be groomed first, saving the "show side" for last. Once both sides have been groomed, the part should be made. The part will be roughed in during the brushing process, but it will have to be finished and made perfectly straight. This is most easily accomplished by using a knitting needle. Starting from the eyebrows and working back to the tail, the needle should be slid under a two-inch section of hair. The needle should then be lifted up away from the dog's body with a slight, wiggling motion. This will make a straight part and allow the hair to fall easily to either side. Then the next two-inch section should be parted and the procedure repeated until the part is complete. The backbone should serve as a guide when making the part. Once the coat has been parted completely, both sides should be sprayed with coat dressing to set the part and hold it in place for the show ring.

The feet and lower legs should be trimmed to make the outline appear neat, and hair should be removed from between the pads of the feet. A small amount of coat dressing may be rubbed onto the leg hair to make it glisten and bring out the tan coloring.

The final touch to the head is to smooth the cheek and muzzle hair and make it lie flat. If the hair on the muzzle is allowed to become rumpled, it will give a false impression of the true quality of the head. Plucking some of the hair from around the eyes will give the proper balance to the head.

The tail of the Silky Terrier should be trimmed of excessively long hair. Thinning shears may be used to avoid too precise an outline.

While in the ring, the exhibitor will find that he must brush the dog after each gaiting to give the coat its typical, neat appearance. When the dog has been pre-ring groomed properly, it will be only a matter of passing the comb through the coat to make all the hair fall the way it should.

A study of two dogs owned by
Dr. Robert J. Berndt, showing
topknots and ear trimming.

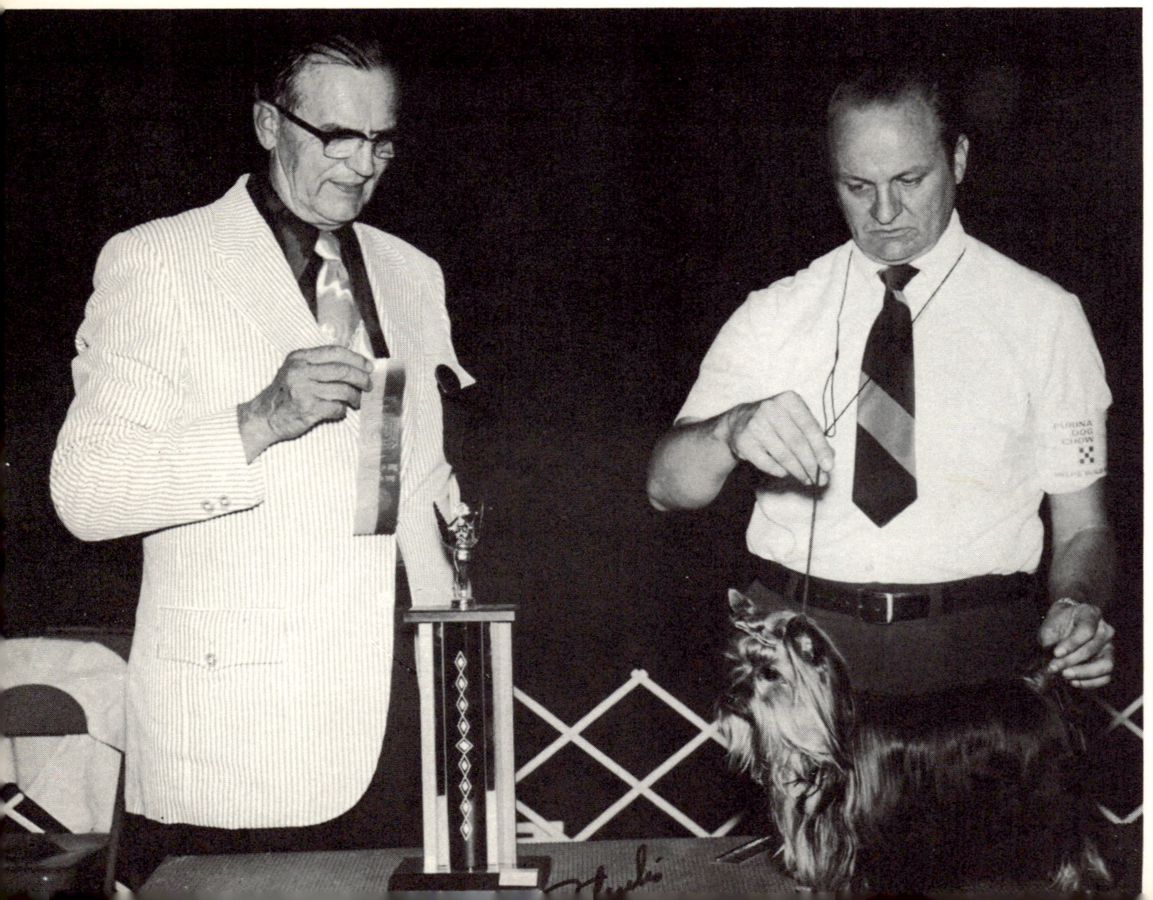

Ch. Yorkfold on Target,
Yorkshire Terrier, owned by
Dr. Robert J. Berndt.

The long-coated Toy dogs are the Maltese, the
Pekingese, the Shih Tzu, and the Yorkshire Terrier. The beautiful floor-length coats of these
dogs attract the attention and interest of dog
admirers everywhere. A dog with a neat, full
coat is a truly remarkable example of his breed,
while, in contrast, a dog whose coat has not
been cared for not only is unattractive but also
is unsuccessful in the show ring.

To keep a coat healthy, one must keep it
clean. A coat that is allowed to become dirty
will tangle quickly and will develop small mats
which will either break the hair or cause it to be
broken in working out the mats. If the coat is
dirty or sticky or caked with mud—which is
often the case when the dog is allowed to run
freely in the yard—the dog should be bathed
thoroughly before being brushed. A partial
bath or even a partial rinsing can save needless
work and worry. It is to be remembered, however, that the hair is in its weakest condition
when it is wet, and it can, therefore, be damaged easily. Careful grooming will be required
while the coat is wet.

With proper training, the adult dog will lie still
on his side so that the underside can be groomed
easily, and the groomer can use both hands in
working on the stomach and under the legs
where mats can develop rather quickly. Care
must be taken to groom from the skin out. Many
inexperienced groomers do not get out the tiny
mats next to the skin, and these mats will destroy the outer coat as it becomes entangled.

The following grooming techniques can be
used on all four of these long-coated breeds.
Under the special section on the Pekingese, an
alternate grooming method for treating body
coat will be described. The description of the
treatment of topknots and head grooming will be
included under the individual breed sections of
this chapter.

With the dog lying on his side, the groomer
should begin under the muzzle, pushing the hair
back. Then gradually, layer by layer, he should
line-brush the hair toward himself with a small,
stainless steel pin brush. Large mats can be detected easily, but small mats are felt only by the
pulling pressure on the brush. When small mats
are encountered, one should work the mat out
with the fingers or with the single tooth of a
comb, pulling one hair loose at a time, if necessary, to avoid breaking the hairs.

On a long-coated dog, some groomers prefer
to use a slicker brush on certain areas such as
the legs and feet. Great care must be taken

Chapter 5

Long-
Coated
Toy
Dogs

when using the slicker brush, for the teeth are set much closer together and will tend to cut the hair if used improperly. However, if it is used properly on the shorter hair covering the legs, the slicker brush can be an asset in detecting small mats. Again these mats should be worked out carefully. The final step is to go over the entire area with a metal comb. This last step is important, for by the time the comb goes through the hair smoothly, the groomer can be sure that there are no mats left.

After completing the area under the muzzle, the groomer should move to the chest, the underside of the leg, and then to the outer side of the leg. After he brushes the stomach and the lower side of the body and both sides of the rear leg, the groomer should turn the dog on his stomach and repeat the process, moving from the head to the rear and line-brushing up to the part. With the dog still on his stomach, it will be easy to do the tail before moving to the other side and repeating the whole process again.

After grooming the dog a few times, the groomer will discover the ease of the technique, and with practice the length of time required to brush the dog thoroughly and carefully will diminish. The regularity of brushing is of great importance in keeping the long-coated dog ready for the ring. With a regular grooming schedule, mats seldom develop and the dog can produce a coat of even length with healthy hair ends.

While grooming the dog, the groomer should use a small amount of hair conditioner or a diluted creme rinse spray, either of which will help to cleanse foreign matter from the hair ends and to prevent damage. A number of hair conditioners made especially for dogs are available in pet stores. Coats react differently to a given conditioner, so it is wise to experiment early on the puppy coat or on the underside of the dog in order to find the most successful spray for a particular texture of coat.

The Maltese, the Shih Tzu, and the Yorkshire Terrier require the body part, but the Pekingese does not. While a part in the hair down the middle of the back of the dog is natural, since hair that length has to fall to one side or the other, a straight line part is something that must be made by the groomer. The easiest way to get an even part after the dog is completely brushed is to use a knitting needle. Starting at the head and moving toward the tail, the groomer can part a two- or three-inch section at a time, sliding the needle down the backbone and then slowly drawing it up, allowing the hair

to fall to either side. When the part is finished and straight, its entire length should be sprayed lightly with water in order to hold the hair in place.

To grow a "Specials" coat on a Maltese or on a Yorkshire Terrier, the coat must be wrapped. Some Shih Tzu owners prefer not to wrap the coat, while many others believe that wrapping the coat is the only way to make it grow floor length and to keep the ends from breaking. Most Pekingese exhibitors do not wrap their dog's coat. However, owners of "Specials" dogs do frequently wrap the coat on the rear so that it will grow longer than floor length and will trail behind the dog when he gaits.

Owners use different types of materials for wrapping, ranging from wax paper and plastic refrigerator wrap to nylon net. The latter, however, is a little too harsh for the soft, silky coats.

Wax paper or butcher paper is the most easily handled and most convenient wrap that can be used. The paper should be cut into strips about four inches wide and one-half inch longer than the hair to be wrapped. The top should be folded down one-quarter inch to make the top edge extra thick and smooth so that the hair will be well protected. The paper should then be folded in thirds lengthwise. Enough wraps should be prepared in advance to wrap the entire coat.

The dog should be brushed completely before sectioning the hair for wrapping. Each section must be combed before slipping the hair into the folded section of the wax paper. The paper is then folded once more lengthwise around the hair. The long thin packet is folded in half and then in half again and held with a rubber band. The edge of the packet should be about one-half inch from the body. Each packet will have to be unwrapped and brushed either every day or every other day, depending on the texture of the coat. If the coat mats quickly, it will have to be brushed daily. The paper wraps can be reused but should be replaced as soon as they begin to wear.

The topknots will be done in a single packet and held with a rubber band. The jaw whiskers on each side will be held in a single packet, with the cheek whiskers in another packet. A single packet can contain the chin whiskers. Two or three packets, one above the other, will be needed for the front of the dog.

Depending on the density and the length of the side coat, the groomer will use either a single row of four packets or a double row, one

A Yorkshire Terrier in wraps to protect the hair. The same sectioning is used on the Maltese coat.

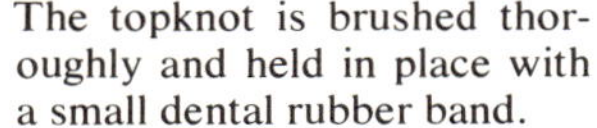

The topknot is brushed thoroughly and held in place with a small dental rubber band.

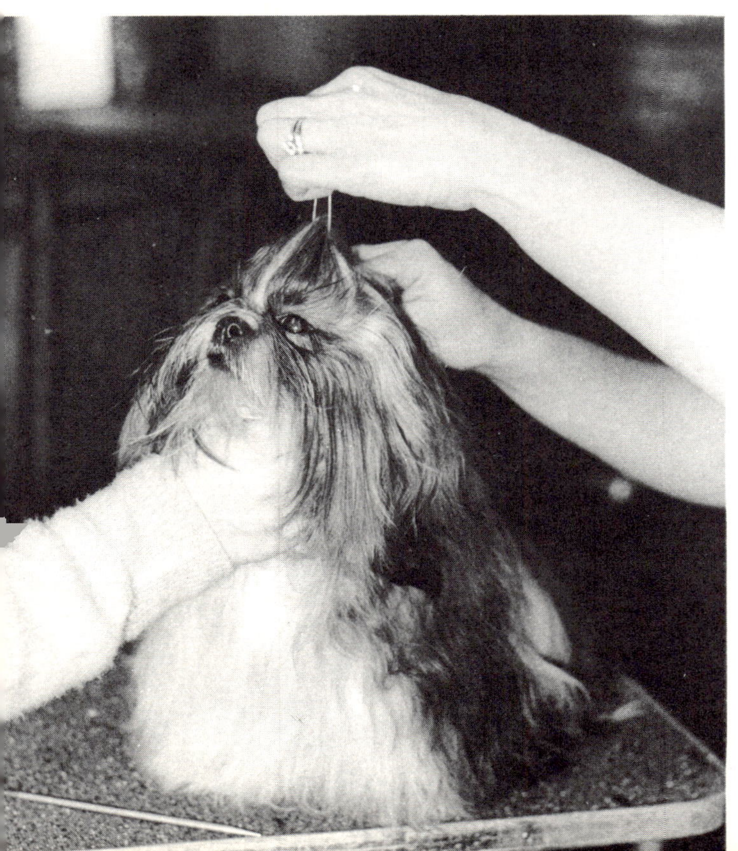

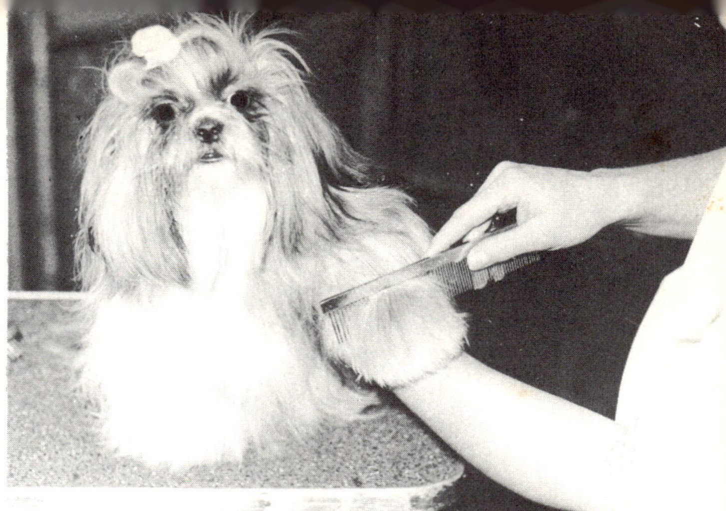

The leg hair is combed straight out before being trimmed to floor length.

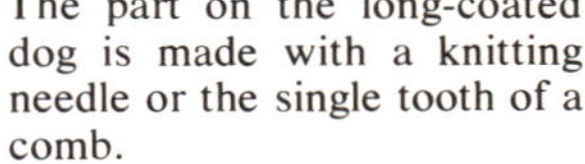

The part on the long-coated dog is made with a knitting needle or the single tooth of a comb.

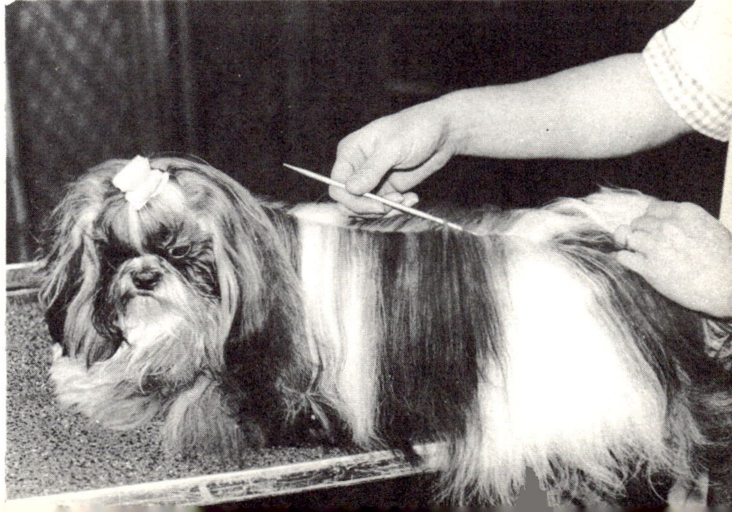

being set high on the side and the other lower to catch the hair on the underside. The front and back packets are formed directly above the legs, while the coat in between is held in two packets. Each side of the neck requires a single packet. The tail will be held in either one or two packets, depending on the length and thickness of the coat.

On the day of the show, the handler should groom the right side of the dog first, saving the "show side" for last. After each layer of brushing, the coat should be sprayed lightly with a diluted creme rinse or a diluted coat dressing to help keep the hair from flying and to keep it straight and in place for each succeeding layer.

Maltese

Staining under the eyes is a problem with white dogs. Minor stains may be treated with boric acid powder and fuller's earth, mixed in equal parts, to which a little water has been added to make a paste. This paste should be applied to the stained hair and allowed to dry. Treatment may be repeated daily after first brushing out any residue left from an earlier application. For more severe staining, a veterinarian should be consulted, for there are several products he may prescribe that can be given orally to prevent tearing.

The Maltese coat, like the Yorkshire Terrier coat, is very fragile and silky and requires great care to bring it to "Specials" condition. From early puppyhood the Maltese coat should be brushed regularly to keep it mat-free and to encourage it to grow evenly into a luxurious full coat. As an adult dog the Maltese will require brushing sessions daily or every other day in order to keep the coat free from mats. The frequency of the brushing will depend on the quality of the coat and its tendency to mat. Care in brushing is of utmost importance. A straight downward movement of the brush, starting at the skin and continuing through the ends of the hair, is very important so as not to snap off the ends.

The coat should not be brushed dry. A mist of diluted creme rinse should be sprayed lightly on each layer as it is brushed, or an aerosol spray containing lanolin or a coat dressing can be substituted. Dampening the hair protects the ends and makes brushing easier. If the brush does not move freely in a downward stroke through the hair, each layer should be teased lightly and gently with the brush, using several downward strokes, until the tangles are gone and the brush moves freely through the coat. Any mats should be worked out carefully with the fingers and brush. While the coat of the Maltese does not break readily, the brushing will be done more easily if the coat is kept clean.

A good grooming routine should include a weekly bath followed by a treatment with a hair conditioner. A mild soap should be squeezed gently through the coat without too much scrubbing—so as to avoid creating mats in the hair. This should be followed by a thorough rinsing. By using a dry towel, excessive water can be blotted from the coat before applying a hair conditioner. Conditioners marketed solely for dogs are designed to strengthen and repair damaged hair. The conditioner should be applied to the coat and rubbed in gently. The dog should then be wrapped in a towel that has been dipped in hot water and wrung out. This should then be covered with a dry towel. The towel wrap should be left on the dog for approximately twenty minutes so that the full benefit of the conditioner can be derived. The conditioner should then be rinsed out completely and the dog dried in the normal fashion, using a pin brush and drying a small section at a time under the dryer. A conditioner used regularly is very beneficial in strengthening the hair. It also gives the coat a healthy, glossy sheen.

Some groomers believe that the coat will grow faster if it is kept in oil. Some oils come in aerosol cans and may be applied during the brushing session while the coat is dry. There are other oils that can be applied after the conditioner has been rinsed from the coat. Conditioning oil is usually diluted in a one to ten ratio with water. This solution can be poured over the wet dog. It is not rinsed off, but rather brushed into the coat during the drying process. It will take a little longer to dry a coat with oil in it than one without oil.

In bathing the Maltese for show, care must be used to remove all traces of oil from the coat. This may require several soapings. The conditioner should be applied after all soap has been rinsed out thoroughly. If the electric hair dryer is used while brushing the dog, the hair will dry perfectly straight. If a conditioner is not used, then a creme rinse should be applied and allowed to set for a few minutes before the final rinsing. This will eliminate static electricity and allow the coat to hang straight without a tendency toward waving. When preparing the dog for the ring, the groomer can use a diluted creme rinse as a mist while brushing the coat. If the dog has been wrapped, the hair must be moistened a bit more than is the case with a coat that has not been wrapped. A small dryer speeds up this process and makes the hair hang much straighter.

The part of the Maltese goes from the tip of the nose to the base of the tail. The hair on either side hangs straight from the part to the floor. The whiskers, the hair on the ears, and the front and rear coat of the dog are all combed straight to the floor. The hair on the tail is brushed forward following the shape of the tail. The plume lies flat against the side of the dog, blending in with the side coat. The bottom edge of the coat may be evened with scissors to give a neat and finished appearance to the coat.

After the Maltese has been brushed completely, he should be set up on the grooming table for the final treatment of the head hair and the topknots. A horizontal part, made from eye to eye, will separate the hair that is to be brushed down into the chin whiskers and that which is to be brushed upward to form the topknots.

The size of each topknot is determined by the size of the head. Each topknot will run from the center part to the outside corner of the eye and should be square. The outer top corners may be rounded slightly. This hair is gathered and held in place with a white dental rubber band. The rubber band is placed over the inside corner of the eye and at a height equivalent to two-thirds of the distance between the centers of the two eyes. This gives a very nice balance to the head and takes into consideration differences in head shapes. The lower portion of the topknot should be pouffed out gently with the tooth of a comb before the remainder of the hair, wrapped at the fold with a small piece of white nylon net, is folded back and held in place with the final twist of the rubber band. After both topknots have been formed in this manner, the final touch is to add the bows, which should be between one-half and three-quarters of an inch long, depending on the size of the head of the dog. Care must be taken to make sure that both topknots are the same size and shape and that the bows are placed evenly.

Pekingese

The Pekingese and the Shih Tzu differ from the Maltese and the Yorkshire Terrier in that they both have a heavy undercoat. The undercoat for both breeds will require careful brushing because of its density.

Under the general description for the brushing of the long coat earlier in this chapter, it was suggested that coat dressing be used during the grooming process. While many breeders believe that this is the best way to protect the Pekingese coat, others believe that the coat should be brushed dry. Instead of using a liquid while grooming, they use talcum powder or cornstarch to cleanse the coat and to help in brushing out the mats. When either powder or cornstarch is used, it must be remembered that it will all have to be brushed out thoroughly before going into the ring.

Once the coat has been brushed thoroughly as described at the beginning of this chapter, it should be re-brushed, but now the hair should be lifted out from the body to give an added illusion of body width. After the hair from the lower portion of the body has been brushed out and up, the top coat should be brushed out straight and allowed to fall naturally, giving the appearance of a thoroughly brushed, straight coat.

The hair on the side of the neck should be brushed out and forward to create a wider looking head. The ear fringes should be combed smoothly over this extra thickness of hair. The hair on the top of the head should be brushed straight back into a ruff. It should be brushed in such a fashion that it makes the top of the head look flat—which will give the required square look to the head.

The tail hair should be brushed to separate each hair. The tail should then be laid over the back and the hair brushed so that it will part up the back of the tail and fall easily to either side. The tail will have to be brushed in the ring after each gaiting, for the rolling movement of the Pekingese will undoubtedly toss it out of its proper set.

The rear of the dog should be groomed so that the hair hangs straight down and trails behind the dog as it gaits. The advantage of wrapping

Ch. Joanne-Chen's Maya Dancer, Maltese, owned by Mamie Gregory.

Best-in-Show Ch. Masterpiece Zodiac of Dud-Lee's, Pekingese, owned by Ruby Dudley.

the hair of the hind legs is that it protects the hair when the dog is not in the show ring and allows it to grow longer than floor length.

Trimming on the Pekingese is limited to lip and chin whiskers and eyebrows. These should be clipped as short as possible. Slipping a finger under the upper lip will force the whiskers out and make cutting easier. While trimming face whiskers, the eyes should be cleaned of any accumulation. The large eyes of the Pekingese occasionally tear, which increases the tendency for dirt to collect in the inside corners of the eyes. These areas should be cleaned daily to avoid any possible irritation to the eyes themselves.

While the feathering on the feet is not trimmed, the hair between the pads should be kept even with the pads themselves. If the hair grows excessively long, it will impede the gait of the dog.

While in the show ring, the Pekingese needs almost constant brushing. This is not because he has more problems with his coat than any other breed, but rather because of the way in which style requires that his coat be brushed. All the back brushing required to give the compact, broad appearance to the dog is partially destroyed during the gaiting process, so the coat must be brought back to its maximum fullness with a brushing after each gaiting. This grooming technique really becomes an automatic reflex for the experienced Pekingese exhibitor.

Shih Tzu

The Shih Tzu has a coat that is parted down the middle of the back like those of the Maltese and the Yorkshire Terrier. The Shih Tzu also has his hair tied up in a topknot, but his single topknot is finished off in a fashion different from the single topknot of the Yorkshire Terrier. In spite of similarities of the part and the topknot, there are some significant differences between the Shih Tzu and the other two breeds.

The Shih Tzu has the double coat—a fine, soft outer coat and a heavy, woolly undercoat. This double coat will require more grooming time because of the extra quantity of hair. Because it is so thick and soft, the woolly undercoat is somewhat more difficult to groom than the silkier outer coat. These two qualities contribute to a natural tendency for the Shih Tzu's coat to tangle and mat. Mats must never be allowed to develop, for the hair will be damaged in removing them. Even if only a small amount of hair is lost in working out the mat, some of the hair ends will become damaged or broken, and damaged ends will cause the hair to become brittle because of the loss of natural oils. This condition can be offset by spraying the coat with a grooming oil during the time that the dog is not being shown. The coat of the Shih Tzu reacts nicely to the same type of conditioning recommended for the Maltese coat earlier in this chapter.

Extra time will be required in grooming the underside of the Shih Tzu, for the woolly undercoat can easily develop tiny mats next to the skin. Thorough layer-brushing of the coat with the pin brush, followed by combing, will detect any remaining tangles or mats. These mats will have to be worked out one hair at a time in order to save as much hair as possible. The grooming must go down to the skin each time if the dog is to produce a full coat of uniform length. Once a coat has become damaged, resulting in hairs of different lengths, it is more difficult to groom and keep tangle-free. The shorter hairs keep rubbing against the longer ones, making them brittle and finally breaking them. It is always much easier to keep a full coat in good condition than to try to restore a damaged one to prime condition.

Daily grooming is required for many dogs that have a heavy undercoat. These frequent grooming sessions will never permit any condition to develop and get beyond easy correction before it is detected. Occasionally a specimen will be found that does not need daily grooming and still does not have a tendency to tangle or mat. This is really an excellent texture of hair and the dog should certainly be utilized in a breeding program.

The dense undercoat is brushed straight down from the part and parallel to the side of the dog to give the body the broad look which is desired in the Shih Tzu. The undercoat of the Shih Tzu is not used in the same fashion as the undercoat of the Pekingese, where the coat is used to give exaggerated width to the body. The ear fringes and the beard of the Shih Tzu are also groomed to the body and add to the smooth outline of the dog.

The single topknot is treated in various ways by exhibitors, depending on the shape of the head and the tastes of the groomers. One of the methods for setting the topknot is to part the hair horizontally from eye to eye, brushing the head hair back to form the topknot. The hair is then parted from the outside corner of the eye to the inside corner of the ear, and from this point across the head to the inside corner of the other ear. This will make the base of the topknot into a square.

Some groomers feel that this will make the topknot too large and will give a bulky appearance to the head. These groomers will part the hair between the eyes as in the description above. They will start at a point at the outside corner of the eye and make a diagonal part to the center of the head at a point about one-half inch behind an imaginary line drawn between the forward attachment points of the ears. This top point can be moved either forward or to the rear to modify the illusion of head shape that the topknot will create. While some groomers use the triangle, others make the diagonal line into an arc when moving the top point, thus creating a semicircle rather than a triangle. The groomer will want to experiment with these possibilities on each individual dog, for what will look right on one specimen may not look correct on another.

No matter which parting method is used, the final treatment for the topknot will be the same. The hair should be gathered around an imaginary center located about two-thirds of the way back on a center line between the eyes. A white dental rubber band should be slipped over the hair and placed about one-half inch away from the head. With the hair held loosely in this fashion, it is possible to pouf the topknot around the edges, keeping the center shorter to give strength to the finished hair set. Once the pouffing has been finished, the rubber band should be twisted and lapped over one or two more times so that the hair cannot slip out.

The final step in finishing off the topknot is to allow the hair above the rubber band to cascade gently down the back and the sides in a semicircle, allowing none of the hair to hang forward over the front of the head. The topknot can be sprayed with coat dressing to hold it in place.

Occasionally a Shih Tzu will be seen in the ring with a small bow or a pompon decorating the rubber band of the topknot. This fashion trend has not caught on as yet, and it may never catch on.

Yorkshire Terrier

The Yorkshire Terrier, like the Maltese, has a single coat, but the hair of the Yorkshire Terrier is of a finer quality and a more delicate texture than the hair of the Maltese. As a result, great care must be taken with the coat so as not to damage it. The conditioning of the Yorkshire Terrier coat is the same as that described for the Maltese coat earlier in this chapter. As stated in the Standard, the texture of the hair is of special importance. The hair is to be glossy, fine, and silky. This correct texture of hair is not difficult to care for, but all brushing must be done gently.

Some Yorkshire Terriers have extremely dense coats that tend to be woolly. This hair is not so fragile, but it does have a greater tendency to tangle and mat. An excessively woolly coat will occasionally require twice-daily brushings to prevent mats and tangles from forming. Since this is not the correct texture, dogs with this type of coat should not be included in a breeding program.

The tips of the ears should be trimmed free of hair to a point slightly more than halfway down from the tip. The hair will be trimmed to this point on both the outside of the ear and the edges, and the hair should be trimmed from the entire inside of the ear. Most groomers prefer to use a scissors to do this trimming, but there are others who prefer to do it with electric clippers.

The only other trimming done on a Yorkshire Terrier is confined to the feet. The hair is cut out from between the pads so that the dog will have a good grip on the floor when he gaits, for excessive hair between the pads will tend to make the dog slip on a smooth surface. The leg hair that hangs to the floor should be trimmed to floor length or perhaps an eighth of an inch shorter. The hair of the feet should also be trimmed in this way. The feet and leg hair can be trimmed most easily while the dog is in coat wraps, for this makes it easy to see the tan hair and avoid cutting any of the blue body coat by mistake. When trimming the back feet, some groomers prefer to trim the rear half of the hair on the foot just a little shorter, in a fashion similar to that used on the rear feet of the Cocker Spaniel. The hair can be tapered from the center of the back of the foot, where it can be almost a quarter of an inch above the floor, to floor length at the side. This does give a neater appearance to the rear of the dog while he is gaiting.

To form the topknot, the hair is first parted horizontally from eye to eye. The hair under the eyes is brushed forward with the chin whiskers, and that above the eyes is used to form the topknot. The side parts for the topknot start at the outside corner of the eye and go to the inner corner of the ear. The rear line is established with a part from ear corner to ear corner. These four parts will form an area which is relatively square. The hair within the square is brushed up to make certain that there are no tangles and is then gathered together. A rubber band should be placed on the topknot just to the rear of the mid-point of the square. The edges of the topknot should be pouffed out a little, allowing the center to be held shorter to give strength to the hair column that will hold the bow. Depending on the size and shape of the individual dog's head, it may be necessary to move the rubber band either forward or backward a little. This will modify the expression of the dog.

Once the pouffing has been accomplished, the hair hanging above the rubber band should be doubled over backward and held with an additional twist of the rubber band. It is a wise safety precaution to use a second rubber band here in case the first one should break when the bow is put on. The loop of hair that is formed by folding the hair back will be between one-half and three-quarters of an inch long, depending on the size of the dog's head, for the loop should be in the correct proportion.

The bow should be made with a rubber band on the back, which can be sewn on, tied on, or included when the bow is formed. The bow should be between three-quarters of an inch and one inch long. The color of the bow should complement the color of the dog's coat. The bow should be placed on the topknot directly over the original rubber band so as to conceal it.

The side coat should be brushed carefully with either a natural-bristle brush or a pin brush and then combed to make sure that all hair is hanging straight from the part to the floor. The side coat should be trimmed to floor length or just a little longer. An excessively long coat may hinder the movement of the dog, for as it drags and catches on the mat it may give the illusion that the dog is not gaiting smoothly. The easiest way to trim the coat to the proper length is to stand the dog at the very edge of the grooming table with the side coat hanging over the edge. While the dog is being held in this position with the lead, the groomer can scissor the ends of the hair just below the edge of the grooming table. After this final trimming, the dog should again be sprayed lightly with coat dressing and brushed dry. This will remove any clippings from the coat.

Best-in-Show Ch. Charing Cross Ching El Chang, Shih Tzu, owned by Troy Phillips.

Ch. Je-Bil's Myrtle, Affenpinscher, owned by Jean C.
Becker.

The hard coat or Terrier-type coat is not typical of Toy dogs in general. The usual coat on Toy dogs is soft and silky and may or may not be slightly wavy. These soft coats must be protected if they are to mature and maintain their full bloom. The harsh coat is, on the other hand, a very substantial coat that does not require the daily care of the soft coat nor does it need to be so well protected. All coats must receive regular care, however, if they are to be kept in prime condition.

The hard coat in the Toy breeds is confined to the Affenpinscher and the Brussels Griffon. The texture of the hair in these two breeds is hard and wiry. This naturally hard coat has been made even more so because of the tastes of exhibitors who have conscientiously sought to develop an even harder coat than the one that would develop were it left alone.

The Standards for both breeds specify that the coats be hard, dense, and wiry. While coats for both breeds have these same qualities, there is a degree of difference between the two. The coat of the Affenpinscher generally has a slightly harsher texture to it than that of the Brussels Griffon. This may be explained in part by analyzing the breeding program that produced the latter breed.

It is generally accepted that the Brussels Griffon is the outcross of breedings between the Affenpinscher and the common type hunting Terriers of Belgium. As the progeny of these breedings were bred back with similar types and recrossed with the Affenpinscher, the Brussels Griffon came to be identified as a separate breed. The Brussels Griffon was later crossed with the Pug of Holland, so the smooth coat of the Pug was brought into the line. Not only was the shortness locked genetically into the line, but so was the softer coat texture. Since many litters of subsequent breedings produced two types of puppies, a real distinction was drawn between the smooth coat and the rough coat, and the smooth variety came to be called the Brabancon.

The short coats of the Affenpinscher and the Brussels Griffon do not accumulate the dirt that longer coats do, and, as a result, do not require the frequent bathing that either the Maltese coat or the Yorkshire Terrier coat requires. There is also the feeling among many exhibitors that frequent bathing of this harsh coat will tend to soften it too much. In an effort to protect the hard texture, many exhibitors simply do not bathe

Chapter 6

Hard-Coated Toy Dogs

their dogs while they are being shown. These exhibitors confine the cleaning of the coat to frequent brushings and the use of a damp cloth to wash out a sticky type of dirt that cannot be brushed out. They will bathe leg furnishings which are of a softer texture hair and are more abundant. In addition to bathing leg furnishings, some exhibitors will use an oil rinse to protect this longer, softer hair.

Affenpinscher

The Affenpinscher with the correct hard, wiry coat will not require stripping to maintain the proper texture of coat. In the past some breeders stripped the body coat to improve the texture, but very few use this method today. By selective breeding of carefully chosen dogs, the breeder is able, over a period of time, to improve coat texture and bring it to the preferred type. This coat of correct texture is then plucked much in the fashion of the Cairn Terrier coat to maintain its proper quality.

A detailed explanation of stripping will be undertaken in dealing with the Brussels Griffon coat later in this chapter. This same technique could be applied to the coat of the Affenpinscher should such a method be required.

The Affenpinscher has a very dense coat that is relatively short. The coat does not grow evenly over the entire body of the dog, and a mature dog will, therefore, have a shaggy appearance. This is proper and is what is called for in the Standard, for it enhances the monkey-like appearance of the dog. The Affenpinscher coat grows for a period of months and then the dog either "goes out of coat" or "blows" his coat. This means that the coat has died and that it will no longer continue to grow. If left to its natural development, this coat would eventually fall out to be replaced by a new coat. The length of time a coat will grow varies considerably, depending on the individual dog. The coat life may vary from six months to a year or more in certain individual cases. Bitches will frequently lose their coats either after whelping or after going through a season.

Once it has been determined that a coat is no longer growing, it will need to be plucked. This is a grooming technique that is easy to perform and, when done properly, causes no discomfort to the dog. As the dead hair loosens it can be pulled out easily, one or two hairs at a time. If there is resistance to the pulling, the hair is not ready to be removed.

The easiest way to pluck is to use the thumb against the surface of the index finger. This will allow the groomer to hold one or two hairs and pull them easily. It is easy to detect which particular area of the coat will need to be plucked, for that section containing dead hair will have lost a certain amount of its natural sheen. Since the dog is to have a shaggy appearance, the plucking should not be performed in a highly ordered fashion. The groomer should pull a few hairs in one section and then move to another section in order to avoid a pattern that would draw a line or make the coat lie smooth and flat.

Some groomers believe that the Affenpinscher has a double or triple coat rather than a single dense coat. They feel that there is always a good coat ready as soon as the old one has been removed. Others believe that the coat is really a single one at various stages of development. In either case, it is felt that by careful, continuous stages of plucking, a dog can be kept in a show coat all year, and that he will not have to be held out after plucking while he grows a new show coat.

Plucking should be done whenever any dead hair is detected. Dead hair adds nothing to the dog's appearance, and its removal will aid the growth of new hair. The overall quality of the coat improves with the removal of the dead hair.

The trimming on the Affenpinscher is confined to the feet. The hair should be cut out from between the pads, and some scissoring may be necessary around the feet to even up any long straggly hair. This hair should be combed straight down, and then any hair dragging on the floor should be trimmed even with it. This will improve the appearance of the legs and feet when the dog gaits in the ring.

The dog's entire body coat is brushed and combed straight. The technique is to brush the hair to give it body, but not to make it look neat and orderly, for this would counteract the correct shaggy look. The chin whiskers should be combed down from the eyes to form a beard which can then be lifted gently out and away from the face to give a soft, casual appearance to the head.

Brussels Griffon—Rough Coat

The body coat of the Brussels Griffon is stripped in order to make it harder and more wiry. Depending on the rate of growth of a particular coat, the groomer may adopt a "three-three" procedure or one of "four-four." This means that the dog's body is divided into three or four imaginary zones that will be stripped at different intervals over a period of three or four weeks. For the average dog, the four zones stripped over a period of four weeks seem to be satisfactory.

If the body is divided into four areas, the largest and first to be stripped is the back and side coat area. This area extends from the base of the tail to the point of the withers and down to the side of the belly area, and includes the shoulders. The hair is left on the belly to give the necessary depth to the chest area. This hair can be trimmed at a later date, if necessary, to blend in with the side coat and also to avoid an exaggerated under line.

A week or ten days later, depending on the rate of growth of the coat, the second section is stripped. This area is a triangular shaped section starting with the front of the shoulders and moving forward to the occiput. The front demarcation line runs from the point of the occiput back down the shoulders to the humerus-ulna joint.

The third section starts with the occiput and follows the jaw line, behind the ears, to the point under the head where the neck and the head join. This area is to be stripped down to the line drawn across the chest where the front legs join the body.

The last area to be stripped is the area between the occiput and the line drawn from the outside corner of the eye to the back of the mouth and under the muzzle in a straight line to the other corner of the mouth. The stripping should not be brought down any nearer than one-half inch above the eyes. This hair can later be scissored to give the illusion of eyebrows and soften the skull line.

For a coat that grows more rapidly, this four-four technique can be modified into one of three divisions by including the areas at the top and bottom of the neck in a single stripping.

On the Brussels Griffon, the hair of the neck is kept neat with the use of a stripper.

On the Brussels Griffon, the hair on the ears is trimmed and the head hair is combed flat against the head.

There is also the continual stripping method which starts at the rear of the dog and removes a little hair every two or three days until the entire coat has been stripped during a three to four week period. This is perhaps the most satisfactory method, for it presents a very even coat on which no demarcation line can ever be detected since there are really no beginning nor ending lines. When doing the stripping in large sections, care must be exercised that the dividing lines are not clearly defined. There should be a gradual blending, which can easily be achieved by having a serrated or wavy line between the sections.

The stripping comb is a special serrated knife blade set into a wooden or bone handle. There are knives for both the right-handed and the left-handed person. The handle is grasped in the palm of the hand and held with the fingers. The thumb is used to grasp a small section of dead hair and force it against the blade so that the hair may be cut at the skin line. The forward rolling action of the hand gives the necessary force to remove the hair easily. Only small amounts of hair are removed with each cut of the stripping comb. This will eliminate the possibility of causing excessive irritation to the skin.

Should a dog's skin be extra sensitive, it can be rubbed with a medicated salve. Sometimes dogs will develop an area of irritation similar to the razor burn that is the result of shaving the human face too closely. When treated, this condition will clear rapidly.

When the stripped coat has matured, usually in eight to ten weeks after the first section has been stripped, the groomer may need to do a little trimming to blend the area where the stripped coat meets the softer hair. This will occur at the top of the legs and on the underside where the belly hair meets the side coat.

While shagginess is the correct quality of the Affenpinscher coat, it is not acceptable in the coat of the Brussels Griffon. When a dog has been properly stripped and when the stripped and non-stripped areas are correctly blended, there will be no hint of shagginess.

The hair will be cut from between the pads of the feet. The hair of the feet will also be trimmed even with the floor to give it a smooth and neat appearance. The unstripped hair under and on the muzzle will be combed forward to form the beard which gives the quizzical look to the face of the Brussels Griffon.

Brussels Griffon—Smooth Coat

The smooth-coated Brussels Griffon is treated for grooming in the same way as are other smooth-coated dogs. His face and chin whiskers will be trimmed off even with the skin, and sliding the finger under the upper lip will force the whiskers out for easy trimming. The hair on the edges of the ears will be trimmed lightly so that there are no long hairs to interrupt the outline. Hair will be trimmed from the inside of the ear as well.

The body coat of the dog should be sprayed with a coat dressing and then rubbed dry, rubbing only in the direction of hair growth. The occasional hair that stands out after this treatment can be trimmed off. The under line will be trimmed of any hair that destroys the smooth look of the under line and tuck-up. Irregular hair on the tip of the tail will also be trimmed off.

The hair between the pads is removed, and the foot hair is trimmed even with the skin line of the pads. The hair is cut to the edge of the root line of the nails. Nails should be trimmed as short as possible to keep the feet tight and firm.

To make the dog ready for the ring, the final treatment of the coat is to spray it with coat dressing and rub it dry with a rough cloth or brush it dry with a natural-bristle brush. The hair is always brushed in the direction in which it grows in order to protect it from breaking and to give a smooth look to the coat.

Specialty Best-in-Show Ch. All Celia's Winning Trick, Rough-Coated Brussels Griffon, bred and owned by Iris de la Torre Bueno.

Ch. All Celia's Smooth Actor, Smooth-Coated Brussels Griffon, bred and owned by Iris de la Torre Bueno.

A Poodle in the English Saddle Clip.

Poodle

The Poodle is unique among the Toy breeds in that he requires extensive clipping and a great deal of scissoring. The appearance of the Toy Poodle should be that of a distinctive, elegant-looking animal. The clippers and scissors are used to carve out this picture. However, this look which captures the eye of many fanciers is one that requires a great deal of time as well as patience on the part of the groomer.

The Toy Poodle presented without the proper pattern or the proper grooming can be a disastrous sight. Many good dogs have not won at shows simply because of improper grooming which made them appear coarse or bad in movement, or gave a completely misleading picture of their true quality.

The Poodle is a difficult breed for the novice to start with because of all the grooming required by the Standard. But with patience, the desire to learn, and an eye for the correct picture of the breed, even the beginner can succeed. Many novices have undertaken to show this breed, and, after practice in grooming, have developed a skill to match that of a professional groomer.

Coat Care

A dirty coat not only is difficult to brush but also has a tendency to snarl more readily. To help protect hair ends, a dirty coat or one that is sticky should be bathed before being brushed. Some Poodles, even though they have not been bathed for some time, have coats that do not tangle or mat. These coats have a quantity of natural oil which makes brushing them very easy. Some groomers feel that such a dog should not be bathed often, for bathing washes away this natural coat oil.

Coats that do become soiled will require a weekly or a biweekly bath. Some groomers contend that the coat must be bathed every seven to fourteen days because the bathing process stimulates the skin and produces a healthier, faster growing coat. When a coat becomes sticky, there is no alternative but to bathe the dog. If the coat does not become sticky and soiled and the brushing is easily accomplished, then the bath may be postponed.

Chapter 7

Coats Requiring Clipping

Many Poodles need only partial bathing to keep them clean, and the partial bath can be limited to the bracelets or the pack. But regardless of how clean a dog is, there comes a time when a good bath is necessary to remove odor and dandruff.

In growing and maintaining a luxurious show coat, one must be faithful to an established routine. As stated in the chapter on conditioning, the dog must be healthy, must have sufficient exercise and a proper diet, and must be kept clean. The Poodle is trained to lie on his side the same as other long-coated dogs and is also line-brushed throughout the entire coat, using a wire pin brush on the main coat. The pack and bracelets may be brushed with a slicker brush, using the same straight sweep of the brush out and over the ends of the hair. Care must be exercised to avoid flipping the coat upward at the very ends, for this tends to snap brittle ends off. The slicker brush gives the shorter hair a fluffier, fuller appearance.

For most Poodles, brushing every other day is all that is necessary to keep the coat mat-free. At the time the coat is brushed, the wraps are taken down carefully, brushed, and rewrapped. Some coats mat very readily, such as the soft, downy-type coat or the one that is in the stage of transition from the puppy to the adult coat, and daily brushing will be a necessity. A coat that is matting excessively can be dealt with in several ways.

The dog can be put down in oil. Oil makes the brushing much easier, for the mats do not form nearly so readily. The application of oil follows the final rinsing of the bath. The oil solution may be a commercial dog oil mixed according to the directions and poured over the main coat of the dog. It is not rinsed off but simply blotted with a towel, and the dog is dried and brushed in the usual manner.

Many groomers keep the coat in heavy oil while a puppy is changing to his adult coat. Oil is also beneficial for a difficult mature coat, or even while a dog is growing a show coat, because oil does protect the hair ends. If oil is to be used, the dog should be bathed every seven to ten days and given the oil treatment before being dried. Using oil on a Poodle may cause a flaking of the skin or dandruff after a time. When this condition occurs, all oil should be removed from the coat for a period of several weeks or until the condition is corrected. A medicated shampoo or dandruff remedy may be used to relieve the condition. When a Poodle is

taken out of oil, the coat will be very difficult to keep mat-free for several weeks or until all of the oil is removed from the coat and the coat resumes its natural texture. The dog must be brushed regularly during this time. It may be necessary to brush him morning and evening, or at least once a day until the condition is corrected. Some help may be derived by using cornstarch and sprinkling it generously on each layer of hair while the dog is being line-brushed. This seems to draw the commercial oil from the coat faster and stabilize the normal condition more quickly.

Cornstarch is used by many groomers to grow a show coat. It seems to have a slick, almost silicone-type texture and does aid in brushing and in keeping the coat mat-free. It is excellent for white coats that have a cotton-like texture.

Those who prefer not to use a heavy oil may apply a lighter type of oil from an aerosol can. This can be applied while the dog is being layer-brushed. In addition, commercial dog oil may be diluted, using more water than directed, and sprayed on the coat while the dog is being brushed. Varying types of coats require different treatment, so a routine should be established for each individual dog and followed faithfully to keep the coat mat-free.

It is good practice to use something to protect the ends of the hair during brushing, regardless of whether the dog is in oil or not. If the coat is in oil, a light spray of diluted oil applied on the ends will make the coat brush out more easily and eliminate the breaking of snarled ends. If the dog is not in oil, a light spray of diluted creme rinse over the ends helps the brushing process and protects the hair.

The day following a bath, the dog should always be brushed, for it is at this time that the coat has a greater tendency to mat. There are times when a coat mats very easily and a dog will develop deep-set felt-like mats. Such a mat must be worked out gently with the fingers, pulling in all directions to open the mat up and then gently teasing it in an outward direction with the brush or the single tooth of a comb until the mat is completely gone. There are commercial preparations that may be applied directly to the mats that will help ease them out with the loss of only a minimum amount of hair. Some help may be derived from spraying an aerosol oil directly on a mat and allowing it to set for a few minutes before working it out. Cornstarch may also be worked into the mat to help make it work out more easily.

If the coat is only slightly snarled, it is generally more successful to bathe the dog before brushing. Many of the snarls and small mats are embedded with soil, and when it is removed from the coat, the mats will brush out more easily. A matted dog should also have a heavier creme rinse poured over him after his bath, and the creme rinse should be allowed to remain on the coat for five to ten minutes before being rinsed off. The dryer will aid greatly in lifting and blowing the mats out of a clean coat that has been softened with the heavy creme rinse.

Topknot

Wrapping the topknot and the ear fringes is necessary if the Poodle is to grow sufficient length of hair on the head and ears to give a balanced picture in the ring. If not protected, this longer hair gets into the food and into the animal's mouth and eyes, and is broken off to a short length.

The topknot hair should be brushed thoroughly before being wrapped. For the first wrap, a knitting needle is run through the hair on the top of the head, making a part from just in front of one ear across to the front of the other ear. Holding the hair with one hand, the groomer can comb through this portion of hair in an upward direction to straighten and smooth the hair before it is wrapped. Using a piece of soft plastic or similar material which has been precut to be just a little longer than the hair to be wrapped and about four inches wide, the groomer can wrap the topknot, starting close to the skin. The sides of the plastic are folded lengthwise around the hair to make a neat wrap with the hair inside lying perfectly straight. The long wrap is folded in half and then in half again until the packet is between an inch and an inch and a half long. This packet is held securely with a small rubber band. Number 8 rubber bands are small enough to work well on wraps and are readily available from bookstores. The wraps should not be so tight that they pull the roots of the hair but must be firm enough to stay in place on top of the head while the dog is active.

Using the knitting needle, the groomer should make a part on each side of the head, level with the ear and to its corner. This section should then be parted at the back of the ears. This second wrap is secured in the same way the first one was.

Another method of preserving the long hair on top of the head and on the back of the neck is to use small dental rubber bands. Some Poodles object to the wraps on top of their heads, and the following procedure seems to be a good substitute. The hair is parted only as at the base of the first wrap—as described above—and secured by wrapping an elastic band around the hair several times. If the hair is long, it may be necessary to wrap a second rubber band around the hair several inches up from the first one, thus holding the hair in a long pigtail. The second wrap is made the same way as the first one. The two pigtails are then fastened together with a rubber band. The dental latex elastics are much softer and will not break the hair as easily as will regular rubber bands. Some pet supply houses carry the latex elastics, or they may be obtained from a dental supply house.

Ear Fringes

The ear fringes should be combed straight and wrapped in the same fashion as the topknot, being careful to bring the wrap only to the base of the ear leather. To be certain that the ear leather is not gathered into the wrap, it is wise to check with a comb at the top of the wrap. The teeth of the comb should go down through the hair between the top of the wrap and the ear leather.

Many Poodles have a tendency to chew on their ear wraps, especially when the wraps are first used. To prevent this, the wrap can be treated with Bitter Apple, Tabasco Sauce, or even vinegar. A piece of cotton is placed over the plastic wrap and held with a rubber band so that whatever solution is used to prevent chewing will soak into the cotton and remain effective. Some Poodles develop such a bad habit of chewing that none of these products will deter them. If this is the case and the dog is actually chewing the hair off the ears in an effort to remove the wraps, there is an alternate procedure that may make it possible to keep the dog from chewing the ear fringes. That is to eliminate the wraps and simply place a rubber band around the hair just below the ear leather. This will help to protect the fringes and keep them out of the dog's mouth.

With a dog that chews the ear wraps when they are in the normal position, it may be possible to control the problem by bringing both ear wraps up around the dog's neck, back of the second topknot wrap, and securing the two ear wraps with a rubber band so that they are not hanging down. This, however, can cause the hair on the back of the neck to mat more readily as a result of the ear wraps moving around in the neck coat if the dog is quite active.

In addition to that of caring for the coat, another routine that should be established is regular treatment of the toenails, the teeth, and the ears of the Poodle.

Toenails

The foot of the Poodle is to be small and well arched, and short nails enhance this appearance. If the nail is long, it must be cut back, but it must never be cut so short that it is even with the pad. If the vein is cut during trimming, styptic powder will stop the bleeding. The toenails should be clipped or filed once a week to keep them the proper length.

Teeth

Teeth should be cleaned once a week. A tooth scaler may be used, or in some cases a coarse cloth rubbed over the teeth is all that is necessary to keep them clean.

Ears

Ears should also have weekly attention. Hair grows deep inside the Poodle's ears and should be removed gently, a little at a time, by using the tweezers or a hemostat. After removing the hair, a small amount of ointment should be swabbed into each ear canal. This will keep the dog from rubbing or scratching his ears. Ears should be cleaned weekly, using cotton swabs which have been dipped in alcohol or ear ointment. The ears should be cleaned thoroughly. Infected ears should be dealt with on the basis of instructions from a veterinarian.

The Poodle ear leathers are quite heavy and lie flat over the openings of the ears, preventing the circulation of air in the ear canals and making these areas susceptible to infection. Attention to the Poodle's ears should never be neglected, for once an ear becomes infected, it may be very difficult to clear up the condition.

Show Grooming

Many groomers prefer to clip the dog before bathing him for show. This frequently prevents clipper burns if the dog has sensitive skin. If the Poodle is bathed two or three days before the show, the electric clipper work may be done at that time. Clipping three days ahead of showing gives the hair a chance to grow back enough to give a smooth, velvety look to the skin of the shaved places. A Number 40 clipper blade should be used when clipping this far in advance, and care should be taken to avoid burning the skin. If a Number 15 or a Number 30 blade is used, the clipping will probably have to be done two days or even one day before showing in order for the shaved places to look neat the day of the show.

Practice in using the clippers is the only way to achieve a really neat looking job. Most groomers clip in the direction opposite to that in which the hair grows. This will give a closer and neater appearance.

Some dogs have sensitive skin that may become irritated when it is clipped. This is called clipper burn and is the result of using a dull blade in the clipper or using too much pressure while moving the clipper over the skin. The condition is not serious and can be compared to a razor burn a man may receive while shaving. To relieve clipper burn, the groomer should apply a medicated ointment to the affected area immediately after clipping.

There are three patterns in which a Poodle's coat may be clipped if he is to be shown. They are the Puppy Clip, the English Saddle Clip, and the Continental Clip. Clipping and scissoring for each of these patterns will be explained in detail later on in this chapter. Here the distinguishing features and the general procedures pertaining to the three clips will be discussed.

The Puppy Clip may be used only while the dog is under twelve months of age. This clip requires that only the face, the feet, and the base of the tail be clipped. After the Poodle is twelve months of age, he must be shown in either the English Saddle or the Continental Clip.

When starting to clip, the head should be held in a secure position with one hand. A line is clipped even with the outside corner of the eye straight to the level of the ear, beginning at the ear and continuing outward to the corner of the eye. Then a half "V" line is clipped beginning at the bottom of the ear and extending to the middle of the throat, well above the breastbone. On the other side of the head a line should be clipped from the ear to the outside corner of the eye and then a line from the bottom of the ear to the middle of the throat, completing the other half of the "V," so that the Poodle's throat is clipped in a "V" pattern ending in the middle of the throat well above the breastbone. This "V" line may be moved up or down, depending on the length of the individual Poodle's neck.

The Poodle's neck is to be well proportioned with length to allow high head carriage, and a short neck would destroy the desired effect. If the Poodle has a short neck, the "V" might be carried down a bit farther to give the appearance of more neck. At this point all remaining hair inside the "V" should be cleaned from the throat, clipping against the growth of the hair and continuing upward until all lower portions of the head have been trimmed. In clipping around the lips, the skin may be pulled tight with one hand to make clipping in the creased area of the lips easier.

The muzzle remains to be clipped, and clipping should begin in the middle of the head between the eyes. A small inverted "V" should be clipped between the eyes, just above the inside corners. The clippers should be used so that they start at the small inverted "V" and move outward to the end of the muzzle. This pattern is followed, clipping forward until all remaining hair on the muzzle is removed. Clipping against the hair growth may make it necessary at times to clip inward or upward on the muzzle, as the direction of growth changes. The groomer should take care to avoid causing clipper burn.

When clipping the feet, the groomer should start at the back of the foot and clip the hair inside the foot pads with an in and out scoop of the clipper. The back of the foot is clipped from the pad upward to a point that will expose the entire foot of the dog, continuing to clip upward to the same point around the foot—leaving only the toe area to be done.

The toes are then spread apart by holding the foot with one hand and using a finger underneath the foot to spread open one toe at a time. Starting at the end of the toe on one side, the clipper moves upward, over the top portion of the toe and down the other side, using the same motion. All toes are clipped in the same manner. When starting to clip, it may be necessary to remove excess hair from around the nails with a small cuticle scissors to make the foot look neat.

After the feet have been finished, the front legs of the Poodle are clipped, leaving enough hair on the bottom of each leg to form a bracelet that will be in balance with the rest of the dog. The leg, from the top of the bracelet, should be clipped up to a point just below the elbow. The front legs of the dog are clipped only if the pattern is to be the Continental Clip or the English Saddle Clip. In the Puppy Clip the legs are left full.

If the English Saddle Clip is to be used, the crescents are set after trimming the legs. A half-moon shape is located on the side of the dog, directly behind the ruff in a position approximately midway between the top line and the under line of the dog.

The base of the tail may then be clipped. If the tail is the correct length, over two-thirds of the hair on the tail should be left to form the pompon. If the tail has been docked too short, the groomer may not be able to clip up that high and leave sufficient hair for the pompon. If the tail has been docked too long, either re-docking the tail or clipping up slightly higher may help to make it look more balanced.

The area on the stomach of the dog should be clipped, using a Number 15 blade so as not to burn the tender skin. The stomach area should be clipped regardless of the style of clip chosen. This is especially important on a male dog, since clipping will facilitate keeping the hair clean in this area.

The only area left to trim on the English Saddle Clip is the band line separating the bracelets and the pack on the back legs. Unless the band line is relatively plain to see from recent clipping, this is best done after the scissor work is almost completed on the bracelets and the pack in order to determine where the band should be. The band between the two bracelets should be approximately one-fourth of an inch wide, as should the band between the top bracelet and the pack. These bands give a distinct separation from the pack to the bracelet and between the two bracelets.

On the face, the feet, and the front legs, the Continental Clip is set in the same manner as is the English Saddle Clip. The rear is clipped starting from just above the hock but leaving sufficient hair for a bracelet. The clipping will go to the main ruff of the coat, removing all hair on the legs and back and up to the point where the pompon on the tail begins. Rosettes are optional on the Continental Clip. For the rosettes a rounded patch of hair should be left high on each side of the hip.

Bathing

In preparing a Poodle for show, a bath is absolutely necessary. Generally the Poodle should be bathed three to five days before the show to allow some of the natural coat texture to return, since a bath does tend to soften the coat. A white dog, however, may have to be bathed the day before the show to look his best. The dog is to look sparkling clean but still have texture to his coat. One way to accomplish this is to bathe the dog from three to five days before the show, and then the day before he is to be shown, to re-bathe the pack, the bracelets, and the tail. This gives a fresh, clean look to the animal and yet will keep texture in the main part of the coat. The same procedure is used in bathing the Poodle for the show as for general everyday grooming.

The clippers are used on the face, starting between the eyes.

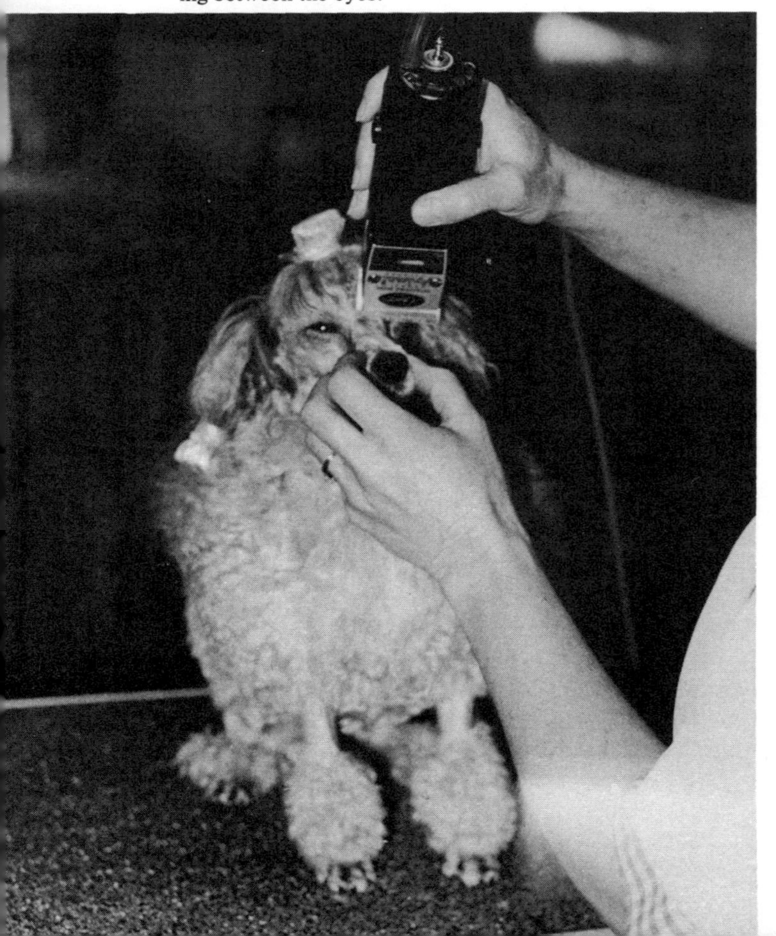

The feet must be trimmed of all hair.

If the dog has been in oil, it may be necessary to use three soapings to remove all traces of oil. After the shampoo has been rinsed completely from the coat, a diluted creme rinse should be poured over the entire coat, followed by a thorough rinsing with plain water. This aids in eliminating static electricity from the coat. The same procedure is followed for drying as is described in the chapter on long-coated dogs.

Some groomers prefer to dry the pack and the bracelets first because this coat is shorter and tends to dry faster. The purpose is to make the hair as straight as possible by drying one area thoroughly before proceeding to another area. Generally the head and ears are dried last and then wrapped. If the hair is not dried thoroughly while it is brushed, it tends to wave or curl and detracts from the overall straight look. After the dog is completely dried, it is a good practice to lay him on his side and completely re-brush through the coat to be certain the coat is thoroughly brushed out. This helps to straighten any hair disarranged from the drying process.

After a day or two some of the hair may tend to wave slightly. The coat can be re-straightened if the groomer uses a water spray while brushing the ruff. Since short hair has more of a tendency to curl and droop, the groomer may prefer to bathe out the bracelets and the pack closer to the time of the show.

If the groomer prefers a curly look to the pack, he does not brush the pack while it is drying. Before drying the short hair, the groomer combs out the pack completely. Then with a comb, starting at the bottom of the pack, he combs the pack gently, pulling out from the body and working upward and over the back. Doing this makes the hair stand out from the body and forms soft curls. Each day the pack must be wet with a water spray and lifted up and out with the comb and recurled. At this time the stray ends of the curls are scissored off to give a smooth, curly look. Some groomers use a steaming towel over the pack each day instead of the water spray to form soft curls.

A good habit to develop is to brush the right side of the dog first. The reason for this is that the exhibitor remains on the right side of the dog, leaving the left side always visible to the judge. If the left side is brushed out last, it generally looks better, for the dog does not lie on it after it has been brushed.

A head study of a Poodle with an "old-fashioned" trim. Hair this length is no longer permitted by the Standard.

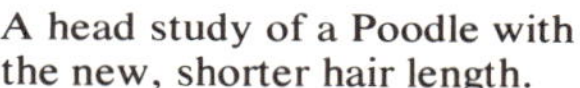

A head study of a Poodle with the new, shorter hair length.

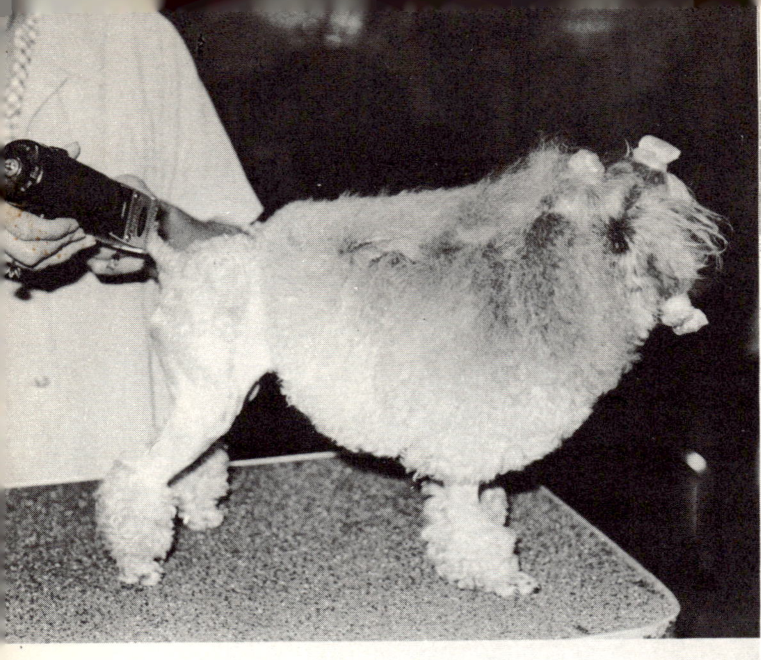

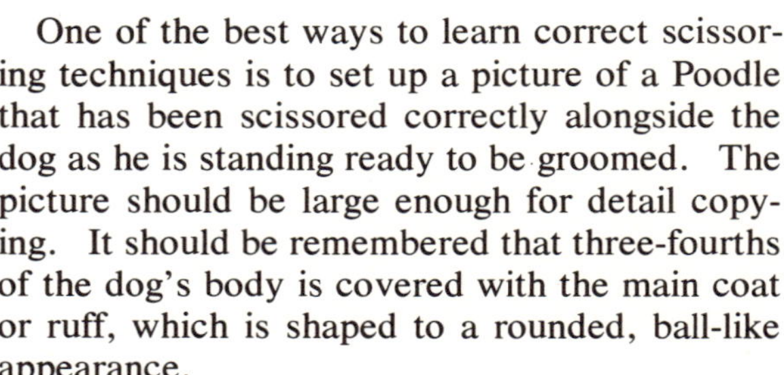

The tail is shaved from the base to the bottom of the pompon.

Scissoring

Immediately following the bath is the best time to scissor the coat. At this time the hair is straightened properly and scissoring produces the blunt ends which make the coat hold its shape longer. If the pack and bracelets are to be re-bathed the day before the show, only the main coat is scissored immediately following the bath.

One of the best ways to learn correct scissoring techniques is to set up a picture of a Poodle that has been scissored correctly alongside the dog as he is standing ready to be groomed. The picture should be large enough for detail copying. It should be remembered that three-fourths of the dog's body is covered with the main coat or ruff, which is shaped to a rounded, ball-like appearance.

The coat of the Poodle should be brushed thoroughly before being scissored. The coat on the back of the neck is brushed straight upward. The rest of the coat on the back is brushed up and slightly forward toward the neck. The coat is brushed this way about half-way down the body so it blends in with the rest of the side coat which extends straight out from the body and blends in gradually with the coat on the bottom of the ruff.

The groomer tries to create the rounded-ball look by the way he brushes the coat. It is good if the dog shakes before being scissored so as to even the coat naturally. Some groomers use hair spray in layer-brushing the coat to keep the hair in place for its rounded-ball shape. Some judges permit this, but many do not like the use of hair spray. When the hair is of the correct

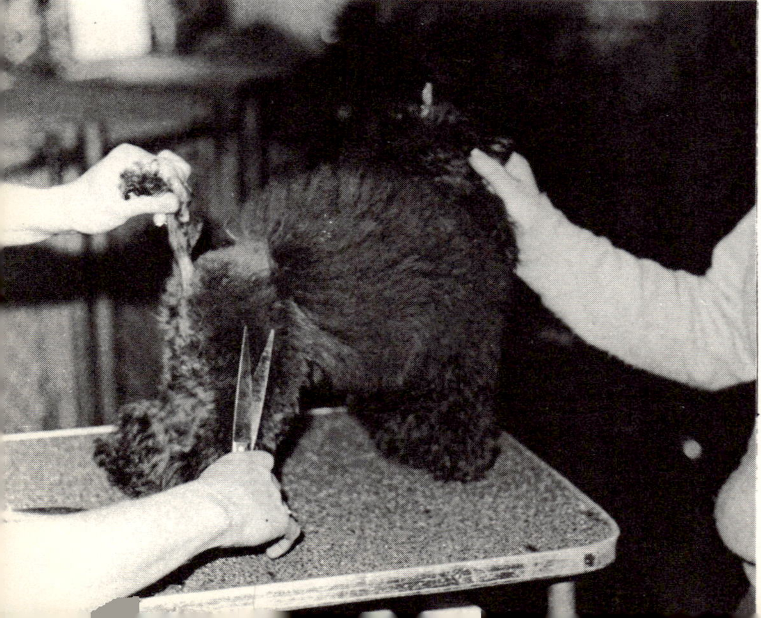

The pack and the ruff are scissored with a smooth action of the whole arm rather than just with the action of the wrist alone.

A Poodle in the Puppy Clip.

texture it is not necessary to use hair spray to keep it in place.

Starting at the bottom of the main coat, a neat under line is scissored. Enough room should be left to allow for the leg area to show to some extent between the front bracelets and the main coat. If the dog has an excellent front and straight front legs, the groomer will want to emphasize this fact by raising the under line of the main coat a bit higher to expose more leg area, thus calling attention to this quality. The groomer starts scissoring upward in a gentle curve to start forming the ball. It is better not to take too much hair off at first, but rather to stand back and compare the work with the picture being copied. The scissoring should create a balanced effect.

For a dog that is longer in body, an illusion of a shorter body can be created by letting the ruff of the coat or the ball extend farther back. Less body extending from the main coat creates the illusion that the dog is shorter in body. Normally, on a well-balanced Poodle, the line of the ruff begins just back of the last rib.

The front bracelets should also have a rounded, ball-like appearance, and this is ac-

complished by scissoring the bottom line of the bracelet to expose the foot sufficiently so that the judge can see it. The height of the front bracelet should be approximately the same as that of the bottom back bracelet in order to add balance to the dog. Many exhibitors feel that if the bracelet is left quite long on a Poodle with a

A Poodle in the Continental Clip.

poor foot, the judge will not notice this defect. This in most cases is not true, for the longer bracelet calls attention to the fact that the foot is covered and the judge is likely to be tempted to raise the hair to look at the foot. Thus the foot probably will get a closer examination than if scissored correctly. However, just a slight bit more length may be left on the bracelet for a dog with a poor foot, but not enough to call attention to it. On an animal with an exceptionally good foot, the groomer may scissor the bottom of the bracelet just a bit higher than normal to call attention to this fact.

After the bottom line of the bracelet is scissored evenly, the cutting edge of the scissors is curved upward to start the ball-like appearance of the bracelet. The middle of the outside section of the bracelet is scissored flat, followed by a gentle curving line to complete the top part of the bracelet. After the bracelet has been scissored the first time, it is re-brushed and combed out, bringing the hair outward from the leg in its natural position. The ends are then re-scissored to make the bracelet look neat and professional.

The hair on the tail is brushed and combed into its natural position and scissored to a rounded ball that balances in length and width with the rest of the coat. The pompon on the end of the Poodle's tail should be scissored to approximately the same height as the dog's head when carried up.

Puppy Clip

The Puppy Clip is full over the entire body, with only the feet, the face, the neckline, and the base of the tail clipped. The body coat of the puppy may be shaped slightly on the rear and on the legs. Just above each foot the bottom line is evened and then a slight curve is scissored to the outside as if making a bracelet. However, after making the first curve, the scissors are kept flat all the way up the leg.

On the front legs the flat line blends in with the main body coat. On the back legs the flat line starts a curve over the rump of the puppy and gradually blends in with the body coat. From the rear it is permissible to scissor a bit shorter so as not to give the puppy a long-bodied look. Using a picture as a guide, the scissoring line is gradually curved over the base of the tail to blend in with the body coat.

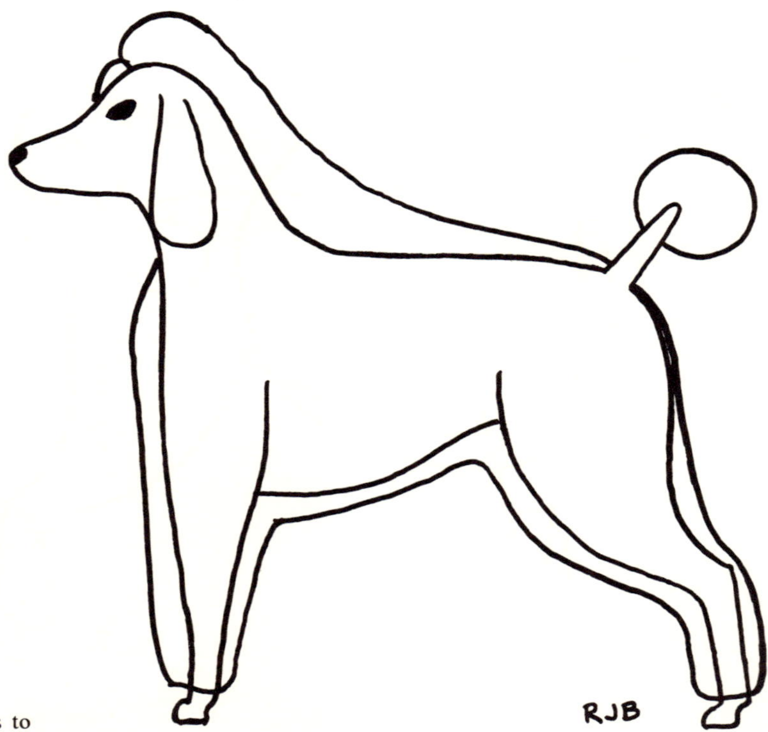

A chart showing the areas to be clipped for the Puppy trim.

Continental Clip

To wear a Continental Clip, a Poodle must have a good rear and should be well angulated. A rear that is not well angulated looks quite straight in this pattern, so the fault is accentuated. This type of clip may tend to give the illusion of a shorter body as a result of the clean line of the rear, since there is no hair protruding. The Continental Clip is used well on a dog that does have sufficient angulation but happens to move close going away. The shaved rear legs give the impression that the dog is moving wider since there is no hair on the inside of the legs.

Rosettes are optional for the Continental Clip. They may appear to give the animal a bit more elegance and many people prefer them. If there are to be rosettes, the hair is brushed and combed out from the body and scissored until there is a rounded, ball-like appearance. The rosettes should be balanced in size with the rest of the coat.

The bracelets on the back legs should be shaped by first making a neat under line. They are then shaped with the scissors more severely upward in the back than the line of the front bracelets. The back bracelets are generally shaped upward at the back of the foot at an angle to the hock, giving the back bracelet an oval or egg shape. The center of the oval is at the tip of the hock. The top side of the oval bracelet is then scissored to match the back side. This seems to add a look of greater angulation and the appearance of a better let-down hock. From the back the bracelet is scissored to look rounded with a slightly oval appearance.

A chart showing the areas to be clipped for the Continental trim.

English Saddle Clip

This type of clip requires a bit more skill than the Continental, but with patience and practice it can be mastered. The main coat and the front and back bracelets are scissored as described for the Continental Clip. With the aid of a picture of a Poodle in the proper English Saddle Clip, it will be noted that the bottom bracelet comes to just above the hock. After this bracelet is scissored in, another of approximately the same size is scissored in above it, leaving about one-quarter of an inch between the top of the bottom bracelet and the beginning of the second bracelet. This is to separate the two and the clippers will be used to create a horizontal band between them. The second bracelet may also be slightly oval in shape and may be left a bit larger than the bottom one. The second bracelet is carved out with the scissors, making a neat under line that curves on the edges. A second one-quarter inch band will separate this bracelet from the bottom of the pack.

A smooth, straight line is scissored horizontal to the dog's body and one-quarter of an inch above the top of the bracelet. This straight line is scissored around the entire leg, gently curving upward on the edges of the pack to follow the shape of the dog's leg. Since the edge of the smooth, straight under line is curved on the outside of the dog's pack, the scissors should develop a straight, flat line upward to the back of the dog and curve over onto the back. The back should be scissored flat. This is easier for some groomers if they scissor flat from the base of the tail upward to the ruff. Shaping should be done around the crescents to make the half-moon trimmed area blend in neatly with the rest of the pack. The back of the pack is trimmed from either side of the dog. Using the scissors, the groomer shapes the hair on the rear of the pack so that it curves slightly upward from the straight bottom line, over the base of the tail, and ties in with the level, scissored hair on the back. The tail is scissored as in the Continental Clip.

The clipping of the bands may be done at this time by holding the clippers straight out from the bracelets and clipping upward between them to create a narrow line around the entire leg. A similar one-quarter inch band is clipped between the top bracelet and the pack. Any stray hairs hanging from the bracelet or the pack are then scissored off. The groomer should stop often to evaluate his work to see if it corresponds with the pattern in the picture.

A chart showing the areas to be clipped for the English Saddle trim.

Grooming at the Show

The exhibitor should arrive several hours in advance of the time the Poodle is to be shown, not only to familiarize himself with the surroundings, but also to have time to groom the dog properly for the ring.

The entire coat should be brushed, using a light mist of coat dressing. Any waves must be straightened in this process by brushing the coat until it is dry. The main coat is scissored again. The bracelets and the pack are brushed out with a slicker brush, and then a comb is used to pull them out to their normal position. At this time the lead is placed around the dog's neck and gathered up under the muzzle and held with a rubber band to keep it out of the way.

The wraps on the ears and the topknot are removed and the waves are brushed out completely, using a spray of coat dressing on them. The ear fringes may be held with rubber bands just below the ear leather to keep them out of the way during grooming. If the Poodle will not hold his head still, someone should steady it so the topknot can be prepared. With a knitting needle a section of hair is parted approximately one-half inch back of the outside corner of the eye, over and around the skull in a half-moon shape, to one-half inch back of the outside corner of the other eye. Holding this section of hair upward, the groomer combs it smooth and then places a rubber band around it at the center of the part line of the half moon. Before wrapping the elastic around the hair, the groomer can bring the hair down slightly toward the back of the skull, for this is the direction in which it should stay.

If the Poodle has an abundance of topknot and it all falls forward in his face, it may be necessary to put another rubber band on the hair. This is done by parting another section of hair directly back of the first topknot, about three-quarters of an inch in width or to the front of the ear. The knitting needle is taken over the skull to the other side of the head to a corresponding point. This section of hair is held upward and slightly back and is secured with a rubber band. On the last wrap-around with the elastic, the two topknots are fastened together securely by flipping the rubber band over the

Best-in-Show Ch. Cutler's Pop Art, Toy Poodle, owned by Nancy Cutler.

first topknot at its base. This is not usually necessary, but on an exceptionally long or soft topknot it does keep the hair up off the face.

The topknot hair is then combed upward and out to give lift to the dog's neck and to tie the topknot hair in with the neck coat. Some groomers use hair spray to help keep the topknot in place. Not only should the hair on the top of the head tie in with the neck hair, but also it should be styled to frame the face of the Poodle and to enhance his expression. If the topknot hair is too long, it should be trimmed to balance the length of hair of the ruff.

With the topknot in place and the dog's coat brushed out for scissoring, the groomer re-scissors over the entire coat, removing any stray ends that might detract from the pattern that was scissored at home. After the ear fringes have been brushed out for the last time they should be scissored to even the ends. Some exhibitors, just before going into the ring, will mist the entire coat of the Poodle with hair spray or coat dressing to help hold the hair in place.

In the ring it is important to maintain the elegant look of the Poodle by combing the hair forward from the end of the ruff to the neck. The topknot should be kept standing up and the ear fringes lying flat along the sides of the head. Each time the dog is moved this will probably be necessary unless the coat is of such harsh texture that it stays in place well. The picture of the Poodle in the ring is one of a very fashionable, elegant dog, and once the groomer has learned to create this picture, he will enjoy a very satisfying feeling of accomplishment.

Long-coated dogs are carried
to the ring in order to keep the
coat clean and neat.

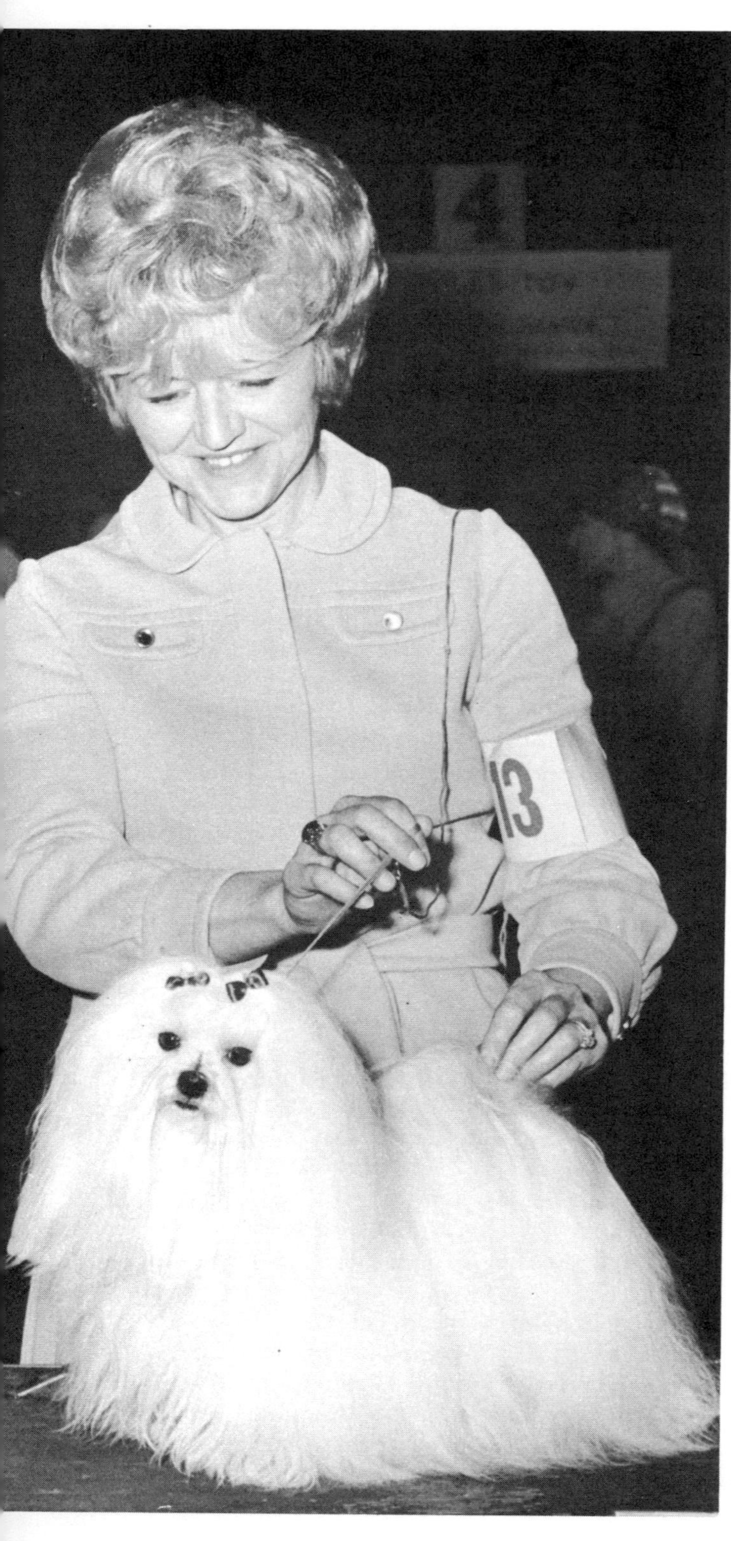

Peggy A. Hogg presenting a
Maltese properly.

Showing a registered dog in competition at a show licensed by The American Kennel Club is the final step in a long process that started with the breeding of a particular litter months before. For the breeder-exhibitor, this experience serves as a testing ground for evaluating the final product of his kennel breeding theory. It provides the breeder with an evaluation of his dog by an impartial judge, and this evaluation should be weighed along with the opinions of other judges and breeders and placed in proper perspective. When enough of these opinions have been gathered, the breeder can then make his own final determination and evaluation.

Early Training

Training and preparation for the ring actually begin months before the dog is ever taken to a dog show. They begin when the puppy is still in the nest. Handling a puppy and "socializing" him are most important aspects of his pre-ring training. The puppy must become accustomed to being handled, not only by the breeder but also by a series of visitors and strangers, and he must be conditioned not to be afraid of strangers. This socializing process which is begun at home is continued over a period of months. After the puppy has received his permanent shots, he should be taken out of the home environment and deliberately taken to places where there is noise and confusion. Public parks and shopping centers are excellent places for socializing a puppy. Here he can have a chance to investigate strangers and to be petted by them. It is really quite easy to find strangers willing to examine a puppy. A simple explanation almost always brings a willing response from someone who stops to look at a cute puppy. The explanation that this is a show puppy that is out to meet the public will suffice. The examiner does not need to be knowledgeable about dogs. Whether or not he examines the dog in the way in which the judge would do it is not really important at this point. The important action is for the stranger to get his hands on the puppy and pet him all over. This builds a pattern and a conditioned response in the puppy that he need not fear the unfamiliar person. This will be of great help when the puppy is taken to his first show.

Chapter 8

Showing the Toy Dog

The puppy not only should be examined on the ground but also should have the experience of being tested on park benches, station wagon tailgates, and just about any other piece of equipment that is solid and will not rock or shake when the dog stands on it. A dog that has met dozens of strangers while still very young will not shy or become disoriented when he is later introduced into the show ring.

Lead Breaking

Another element of early pre-ring training is the lead breaking of the puppy. This must be done slowly and gently for it to be most effective. Putting a leash on the puppy and dragging him when he balks can build a pattern of hate and fear for the lead that may be extremely difficult, if not impossible, to break at a later date.

The first step in the process can be to try the puppy on a show lead. In some cases the puppy will take off and follow the handler with no problems at all. This is most fortunate for the handler, but it is certainly not the case with all puppies. When a puppy does adapt readily to the lead, he should be given very brief fun lessons daily so that he will have the opportunity to set the pattern firmly. The repetitiveness of the training is what locks the comfort and familiarity into the dog's mind and is what makes him feel relaxed and at home in the show ring when he finally arrives at that stage of his development.

If the puppy fails the lead test, a different approach will have to be taken. One method that can be tried is to leave the lead on the puppy and let him walk with it in whatever direction he wants to go. He may stay flat on the ground and refuse to move. Firmness is required here. Just let him lie on his stomach for whatever length of time may be required. The handler can occupy himself with another puppy or do a number of things, but he should always stay within sight of the reluctant puppy. The puppy should never be left unattended with a lead on for fear that he may panic and run, catching the lead on something and causing himself physical harm. Usually the puppy will begin to move after a few minutes, even though it may be a ground-level slink on his stomach. Any movement should bring great praise and attention from the handler.

Once the puppy has started to move with the lead on, the training is well on its way. The first steps are the most difficult. Subsequent sessions have as their goal to get the puppy going in the same direction as the handler and to stay by the handler's side. The first week the handler may be required to follow the puppy until he sees that no harm will come to him. A special enticement can speed up the training process. If the handler is in the habit of baiting his dogs with liver while in the ring, this same method can be used to speed up the efficiency of lead breaking.

For the occasional puppy that refuses to walk with a lead on, a different method can be used. This puppy should wear a small collar several hours each day so that he becomes accustomed to having something around his neck. With time he will begin to tolerate a leash's being attached to the collar. When that time comes, he should be allowed to drag the leash around the yard under the supervision of the handler. From free-leash exercise to controlled-leash exercise is a simple step in the training. When the puppy finally begins to accept the handler on the other end of the lead, then the closely directed lead training can begin in earnest.

When training begins on a very serious note, the show lead should be used exclusively for pattern drills. The pattern drills are those which imitate the exact ring procedures that the puppy will be expected to follow in the ring. The practice of entering the ring, even if it be only the hint of a ring, should be deliberate but relaxed. The dog should be trained to walk on the left side. In these training sessions he should not be permitted to build any bad habits. One action that is seen all too frequently in the ring is the dog's carrying his own lead in his mouth. This forces the dog to turn his head slightly and will not allow him to gait properly. Not permitting this habit to get started is much easier than trying to break it once it is already well established.

The puppy should get in the habit of making square corners and following the speed set by the handler. He should also be conditioned to the fact that the handler may wish to change lead sides on the far side of the ring to avoid getting between the judge and the dog.

The puppy should not receive all of his training from one individual. It is to the advantage of the puppy to be handled by several persons over a period of time. It may become necessary occasionally to have someone other than the trainer take the dog into the ring. If he has had experience with different handlers, this will cause no new concerns for the puppy at the show.

Gaiting the dog is normally done with the lead held in the left hand. The extra length of lead is held in the closed hand so that it does not dangle and annoy the dog. An excessively long lead will permit the dog to stray and allow him the opportunity to weave away from the handler. There are times when a puppy will strain to pull away from the handler. One procedure for correcting this is to hold the lead in the right hand, allowing it to rest across the handler's knees. When the puppy begins to pull away, the handler can use a little knee action against the lead. This very gentle tug is repeated with every step as the knee brushes the lead. The action is so continuous and gentle that it will not break the pace of the dog, but it will keep him going straight down the mat.

In the case where the dog tends to lean into the handler, the process can be used in reverse. The lead should be placed on the left side of the dog's neck rather than on the right side or on top. It can be carried over the dog's neck or under it, depending on which direction he needs to be guided. It will be held over his neck in the left hand, which can be carried directly over the dog's neck or even farther toward the center of the ring to facilitate urging the dog in that direction.

None of these unusual lead techniques should be tried in the ring before they have been practiced at home. The dog should be taught all of them in his adjustment training period. The trainer may never have to use these techniques, but it is much safer to have the dog ready and not need to use them than to need to use them and not have the dog ready.

The dog should be trained to walk on the square, on the rectangle, and on the diagonal. He should be taught that it is also necessary to walk an "L" and at times a "T." Different judges prefer different ring patterns when they examine the gait of a dog in looking for faults.

Not only should different patterns of march be practiced, but also the dog should become accustomed to different ground surfaces and textures. The dog should be taught to walk on concrete, grass, and bare earth. If possible he should also have the opportunity to gait on rubber mats. It is a wise investment for a dog owner to have a piece of rubber matting at least ten feet in length for practice sessions, since most rings use rubber matting.

In gaiting the dog, the handler should see that the dog walks in the center of the mat. Whether or not the handler is on the mat at all is of little importance. Rarely does a Toy dog gait so rapidly that the handler is in danger of slipping and falling. A Toy dog, however, speeding over slippery pavement can show off faults that will not appear when he is in good control of himself. The mat will give the dog good traction and help prevent a sloppy gait.

Standing for Examination

Next to gaiting, standing for examination is the most important pre-ring training exercise for the dog. For a dog to be examined by a judge, he must stand quietly and not shy. This is an absolute essential, for the dog that will not stand for the judge's examination must be excused from the ring. This not only is an embarrassment for the handler but also is a waste of the entry fee.

Training to stand for examination is started about the same time that the puppy is being weaned. While he is being handled to socialize him, he can also be set up in a show stance. This should be a very gentle process and is best started while the puppy is being held in the handler's lap. He can be encouraged into a standing position and praised so that he stays in this position even if only for a few seconds the first time. The time the puppy stays in pose can be increased with each succeeding training session. Not only can the length of time be increased gradually, but also the correctness of pose should receive attention. This whole training process should be made into a sort of game so that the puppy does not feel that he is being disciplined. He should be rewarded amply with praise when he is good and can even be given a tidbit after the session.

From training sessions in the handler's lap to training sessions on the floor is a simple step. The puppy should still feel that this is an easy and natural exercise. When the puppy is being trained on the floor, the posing is accompanied with lead training. These two patterns are now run together just as they will be in the ring at a

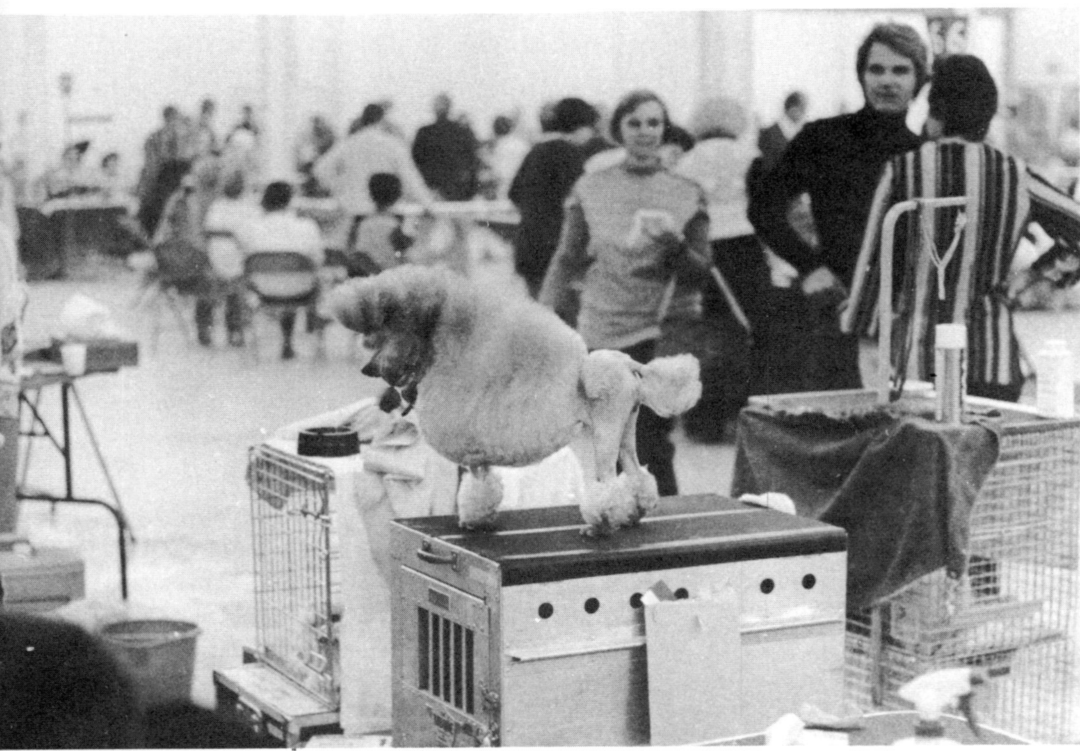

Once the dog has been groomed for the ring, he may be perched on a crate until his class is called.

The dog should always be gaited on the mat so that he will have good footing.

later date. Working the two together will give the real ring experience a comfortable and natural feeling.

After the puppy has been taught to pose on the floor, he should also be taught to pose on the table. Toy dogs are almost always examined by the judge on a table, so the puppy must become accustomed to this procedure. A grooming table is about the same size and height as the show table supplied by the superintendent. Since Toys are frequently examined two at a time on the table, the puppy should become accustomed to being examined at either end of the table with the handler either on the left or on the right. Occasionally a judge examines three dogs on a table at a time, and the handler may have to set his dog up from the rear.

The Toy dog should be set up near the front edge of the table so that the judge can get the best view of the front of the dog. This allows the judge to examine the dog without having to lean over the table and into the dog. It also eliminates the possibility that the judge might move the dog forward to the edge of the table. Some dogs do not like the judge to move them even though they do not mind his examining them.

When the judge takes his first look at the dog, the handler should have the dog posed in a very formal stance. The head is held in position with the lead, and the rear of the dog is controlled by the way in which the handler holds the tail. The judge usually looks at the dog from the front and then steps to the side to get a side view before examining the dog physically. Other judges look at the front and then examine the dog physically before moving to a side examination.

After examining the dog thoroughly, the judge steps back to get an overall view to substantiate what he has found in the physical examination of the dog. In most cases the judge gaits each dog individually after he has examined it on the table. This gives the judge another opportunity to determine that what he has found in the individual examination on the table is proved by the gait of the dog. Some judges examine each dog on the table before gaiting them individually. This is a matter of personal preference on the part of the judge, and the exhibitor should be prepared for whatever pattern the judge wishes to follow.

Some dogs are leaners when they are placed on a table. The leaning habit is one that must be broken long before the dog enters the ring. If the dog leans forward, he should be set at the front edge of the table. His training may even require that he be allowed to slip off the front edge to stop the leaning. The trainer must be extremely attentive to see that the dog is not hurt in this rather drastic training procedure.

While some dogs lean forward, others keep backing up and trying to sit down. These dogs are trained at the rear of the table, allowing them to slip a little if necessary in order to break their backing habit. There are other dogs that will lean sideways, hoping to rest against the handler. These dogs are set up at the side edge of the table, and the slipping process is repeated. This method of training leaners is most effective and usually does not require more than one or two training sessions to break the habit.

Weight Control

In addition to lead breaking and training to stand for examination, attention must be given to the physical conditioning of the dog. The dog's weight must be controlled. This is a process that requires weeks of preparation. Some dogs are good eaters and maintain the proper body weight for their bone and muscle structure. Some dogs are gluttonous and have to be kept on a regulated diet or they become too fat and do not move properly. These two types of dogs cause no great concern for the handler, for their condition is easily maintained or easily corrected.

The dog that causes problems for the handler is the dog that appears to have no appetite. He may eat well at home but will refuse to eat while on a show circuit, or he may just never be very interested in eating and will only pick at his food. Since a thin dog does not win in the ring, this condition must be corrected.

The first step in trying to correct the eating habits is to vary the diet, hoping to find something that appeals to the dog and will increase his appetite. If all else fails, the handler has no other alternative than to force-feed the dog. While this process may be an inconvenience to the dog and the handler, it is to the benefit of the dog and causes him no real discomfort or harm.

Before embarking on a program of force-feeding, the trainer should determine the correct weight of the dog and what weight he should carry. This is in part determined by the requirements of the official Standard of the breed, allowing adjustments for the particular dog to be treated. In the case of a dog where the Standard permits an allowable weight of up to seven pounds, a handler may determine that the dog needs to add a pound or perhaps even more. With a breed where the Standard permits a three pound dog, it might only be a quarter of a pound. This predetermined figure may have to be modified either up or down when the dog finally reaches this weight.

High protein concentrates that are low in bulk seem to be the most effective type of food to be used in force-feeding. A typical mixture could be one of the cellophane-packaged imitation hamburger products mixed with a little ground beef. The mixture should be moistened with a little water and a few drops of polyunsaturated corn oil. Only enough liquid should be added so that the mixture can be formed into pellets. Too much moisture makes it impossible to work with and too little allows the pellets to crumble.

The size of the pellet is determined by the size of the dog—the smaller the dog, the smaller the pellet. The average size for a Toy dog would be about an inch long and about three-eighths of an inch in diameter.

The technique for feeding the pellets is easily learned and causes the dog no discomfort when properly done. The experience is much more traumatic for the handler the first time than it is for the dog. It usually takes only one or two sessions to train both the handler and the dog. It is good training for the handler to watch someone force-feed a dog before trying it himself. Many professional handlers have at least one dog in their string that requires force-feeding. Asking permission to watch the procedure can save a great deal of concern for the novice.

The pellets are usually all made before starting to feed the dog. Some dogs may require only a half dozen while other dogs might require as many as twenty to maintain the proper weight. The pellets may dry out a little by the time the last one is made. In this case each can be dipped quickly in water before sliding it into the dog's mouth. This allows the pellets to go down more easily.

In the case of the right-handed person, the dog's muzzle is held from above with the thumb and the forefinger of the left hand. The head is tilted back slightly. With the thumb and forefinger inserted slightly into the mouth to keep it open, the pellet can easily be slipped into the mouth. The pellet should be placed back far enough in the mouth so that it goes over the ridge that the tongue forms in the back of the mouth. Once the pellet passes this point in the throat, the natural involuntary reflex of the throat muscles will carry it to the stomach. The dog may have a surprised look on his face the first few times, since he is experiencing the eating feeling without the work involved.

Once the pattern has been established, the dog will adjust easily. Some dogs become very lazy and do not want to eat out of a dish at all. They prefer to be force-fed all the time. Other dogs prefer to eat more and skip the extra-food treatment. While the process may consume a great deal of time at first, with practice a dog can easily be force-fed in five or ten minutes.

Weight control is very important for show dogs if they are to be kept in prime condition. An underweight dog will not produce as beautiful a coat, nor will he move as smoothly as he should. If force-feeding is the only way to keep the proper weight on a dog, then this procedure should be undertaken.

The Day of the Show

All actions should be so planned that they are accomplished smoothly and in a fashion that will not make the dog nervous the day of the show. This means that the exhibitor should arrive at the show site several hours before the dog is to be shown. In some cases this may mean arriving the night before the show to set up in the show building for an early ring call. There are several advantages to setting up in the show building the night before. It assures the handler that he will have plenty of room for his crates, grooming tables, and exercise pens. It also has the important advantage of acclimating the dog to the noise and confusion before he must go into the ring. This is good experience for the novice dog, for he will have several hours to adjust to the atmosphere of the show building.

For small dogs that are excessively nervous and keyed up the day of the show, it is wise to provide some special tidbits and perhaps a little honey. Having food in the stomach and an extra supply of sugar will help to restore the energy that nervousness will burn off. The dog should also have an opportunity to drink before the grooming process starts.

In addition to being fed, the dog should be exercised before being groomed. He should be allowed sufficient time in the exercise pen or should be walked on a lead so that he can relieve himself completely before going into the ring. If the dog does not have an opportunity to exercise before going into the ring, he can become extremely uncomfortable and may not gait well nor behave properly. If he does finally relieve himself in the ring, however, he may still have an opportunity to be examined thoroughly by the judge. More than one dog has lost at a show because he was physically uncomfortable and did not behave.

Showing

The actual showing of the dog is the final step in a long training process that began many months before. It should be approached as just another step in a show career. If a handler becomes nervous, he may communicate his nervousness to the dog. As the handler becomes tense, his hands begin to quiver while he is grooming the dog. The dog can sense this change and become apprehensive. The handler further complicates the situation if he fumbles with the lead and over-handles the dog because of nervousness. The handler must control himself if he ever hopes to control the dog.

Showing is a combination of fun and hard work. The pleasure comes from meeting other breeders and exhibitors at the show and in being in competition with them in the show ring. Being able to see one's breeding line in comparison to those of other breeders is also an educational opportunity. The breeder not only receives a professional opinion from the judge but also learns to evaluate his own dog as he watches the other dogs gait in the ring. The judge does have one big advantage that the exhibitor in the ring does not have. He gets to put his hands on all the dogs in competition. Going over each dog is an extremely important part of judging, and especially so in the case of long-haired breeds, for a beautiful long coat can cover numerous imperfections.

The hard work of showing not only involves long hours, hundreds of miles of driving, and sleeping in a different motel every night, but also doing all the backbreaking grooming, bathing, and exercising of the dogs in preparation for a few brief moments in the ring. The time in the ring can also be a strain if it results in a loss. Losses are always a little harder to accept when one is physically tired.

Getting the Toy dog ready for the ring on the day of the show follows the bathing and pre-grooming procedures the exhibitor performed before he left for the show circuit. The coat must be groomed meticulously from the skin out so that there are no skin mats which will destroy the natural outline of the dog. By the time a dog is ready for the ring, he should have been thoroughly trained to lie on his side for whatever period of time is necessary to groom him completely. This training should have been started months in advance so that the dog will not have to be disciplined the day of the show. The handler should avoid those actions which might tend to make the dog nervous before he goes into the ring.

Ring Grooming

On the day of the show, the handler should groom the right side of the dog first, saving the "show side" for last. After brushing the dog, or layering the dog in the case of the long-haired breeds, the coat should be sprayed lightly with water or a diluted coat dressing to help keep the hair from flying and to give the coat a nice sheen. Great care must always be exercised when spraying any preparation—and even when spraying water. The dog's eyes and nose should be covered to avoid any possible irritation.

After the dog has been brushed completely, he should be set up on the grooming table for the final treatment of the coat. With the short-haired dogs this consists of smoothing down any stray hairs and doing the final trimming of the whiskers. With the long-haired dogs it includes making the body part. The groomer starts at the nose and moves back to the base of the tail, parting one small section at a time and using a light spray to keep the newly parted hair in place. After completing the body part, the groomer should return to the head to make the horizontal part from eye to eye which separates the hair that is to be brushed down into the chin whiskers and that which is to be brushed upward and back over the head. The final touches for the topknot depend on the requirements of each particular breed. The final grooming before going ringside is to make sure that all hair is smooth and flowing and that the dog is groomed to show him to his best advantage.

Ringside

Whenever time permits, it is wise to have obtained the armband from the ring steward well in advance. This eliminates last minute confusion at ringside, where there is always a great deal of activity as the classes are entering and leaving the ring. The armband can, however, be picked up just prior to entering the ring. In this case the exhibitor has to arrive in sufficient time to ensure that he is not marked absent.

In order not to delay the judging, the handler should arrive at ringside a few minutes before the class is called. Arriving too early may make the dog nervous if he is forced to stand near the gate with lots of exhibitors and spectators milling about. The Toy dog should be carried to ringside rather than gaited through the crowd where he might get bumped or stepped on.

The short-coated dog can be carried under the arm where he can be protected from any excessive jostling. This would not be the correct way to carry the longer coated dog to ringside, for it would rumple his hair. To lift the long-haired dog from the grooming table, the left arm should be slipped under the dog from the rear. The dog will straddle the arm with his stomach resting firmly on the forearm. The left hand will steady the front legs and support the chest of the dog, giving him assurance and preventing the possibility that he might slip. The dog's lead can be draped around the handler's neck to keep it out of the way. The right hand of the handler can act as a shield to protect the head and to keep the coat in place while moving through the crowd. The dog should be protected from getting bumped during the confusion. As crowds get larger and larger at dog shows, it becomes more and more difficult to get to ringside.

A long wait at ringside can be a problem. Some shows provide tables outside the Toy rings to hold dogs while they are waiting to go into the ring. If there are no tables, however, the handler either has to hold the dog or find a clean place on the floor near the ring where the dog can stand and relax, but where he can be protected. Dirty floors are bad for floor-length coats, but this is just one of the hazards of showing.

Ring Call

When the class is called, the handler should already have determined where his dog will show to the best advantage, and he should then try to get in that place in line if he can accomplish it tactfully. If the dog gaits rapidly, the head of the line would be the preferred position. If the dog moves slowly, however, the end of the line is the obvious choice. A slow moving dog in the middle of the line only calls attention to the fact that he may not move well. The end of the line is also the best place to show the dog that keeps looking back at the dog following him. The handler should take advantage of those techniques which show his dog most advantageously.

Sometimes an exhibitor, in his effort to get into the ring first, blocks the gate so that the preceding class finds it extremely difficult even to leave the ring. Being first in line does not necessarily ensure a win, for the competent judge will find the best dog no matter where he is in line so long as he is well presented.

Setting Up

In the ring the dog should be set up and then worked just enough to keep him in pose. Over-handling a dog tends to make him nervous and prevents the judge from getting a good look at him. The handler should remember that a judge is always looking at his dog. Even if the judge is at the other end of the line, he may look back to see how another dog looks in comparison to the dog he is examining. Allowing a dog to sit or sag can lose a placement.

Obviously there is no perfect dog, for every dog has strong points and weak points. Consequently the strong points should be emphasized and the weak ones minimized. This is not unethical when it is remembered that there is no perfect dog and that all exhibitors have the same set of difficulties to work with. Since the judge will pick the best dog in the class, the exhibitor must prove to him that his dog has more strong qualities than the other dogs in the ring.

If, for example, a dog has a particularly beautiful head, the exhibitor should turn the dog's head toward the judge when he walks past as he is examining the entire line of dogs. Attention can be drawn to a good top line by passing the hand over it with a straight and level motion as the judge is looking at the dog. In the case of a long-haired dog with a full plume tail, the tail can be held aside for a moment so that the straight top line can be seen. Rear angulation can be indicated by lightly brushing the hand down the back legs.

These actions which call attention to the special qualities of the dog should be used sparingly and only when the handler has determined that the judge has not noted the trait properly. If the handler is constantly moving his hands to direct the judge's attention here and there, he may destroy the overall picture of the dog, and the hands may even get in the way of the judge so that he cannot see the true qualities properly. Over-handling is really worse than under-handling. Pushing a dog too hard at a judge may irritate him.

Frank Sabella with a beautifully posed Miniature Pinscher, Ch. Allen's Brandy Snifter.

Ring Procedure

While ring procedure may vary from judge to judge, there is a certain similarity in pattern that an exhibitor may anticipate. When the exhibitor enters the ring, he sets his dog up so that the judge can see him at his best. After the entire class has been assembled, the dogs gait around the ring once or twice. They are then examined on the table and gaited individually. After each dog has been gone over, there is usually a final group gaiting before placements are made. Some judges sort the dogs out for the last go-round while others may pick their choices while the dogs are still in their original order. A judge may even gait one or two dogs individually a second time in order to determine his final placements. The exhibitor should pay attention to the judge's instructions and watch what the other exhibitors do as well.

The individual examination and gaiting provide the best opportunities the exhibitor has to show off the outstanding qualities of his dog. The set-up on the table should minimize the weak points and accentuate the strong ones. The individual gaiting is perhaps the most important moment in the ring, for this is when the judge tests his physical examination of the dog against the dog's performance. While in the line of march, the exhibitor can vary his speed only so much without calling improper attention to himself and to his dog. For the individual gaiting he can set whatever speed is best for his dog. The correct speed in gaiting should have been determined long before the dog was ever entered in a show. Each dog has an optimum speed at which he moves. Moving him at a different pace does not produce the same picture of motion. The dog should gait straight down the center of the mat, neither leaning nor crabbing. He should move briskly but not so fast that he has to break from a fast walk to a run to keep up with the handler. The turns should have been so thoroughly practiced that they are smooth and do not force the dog to change pace to make them. Turning a corner in a slovely manner may give the impression that the dog has a faulty movement when this is not the case. Practicing gaiting between shows, even for the trained "Specials" dog, is well worth the time invested.

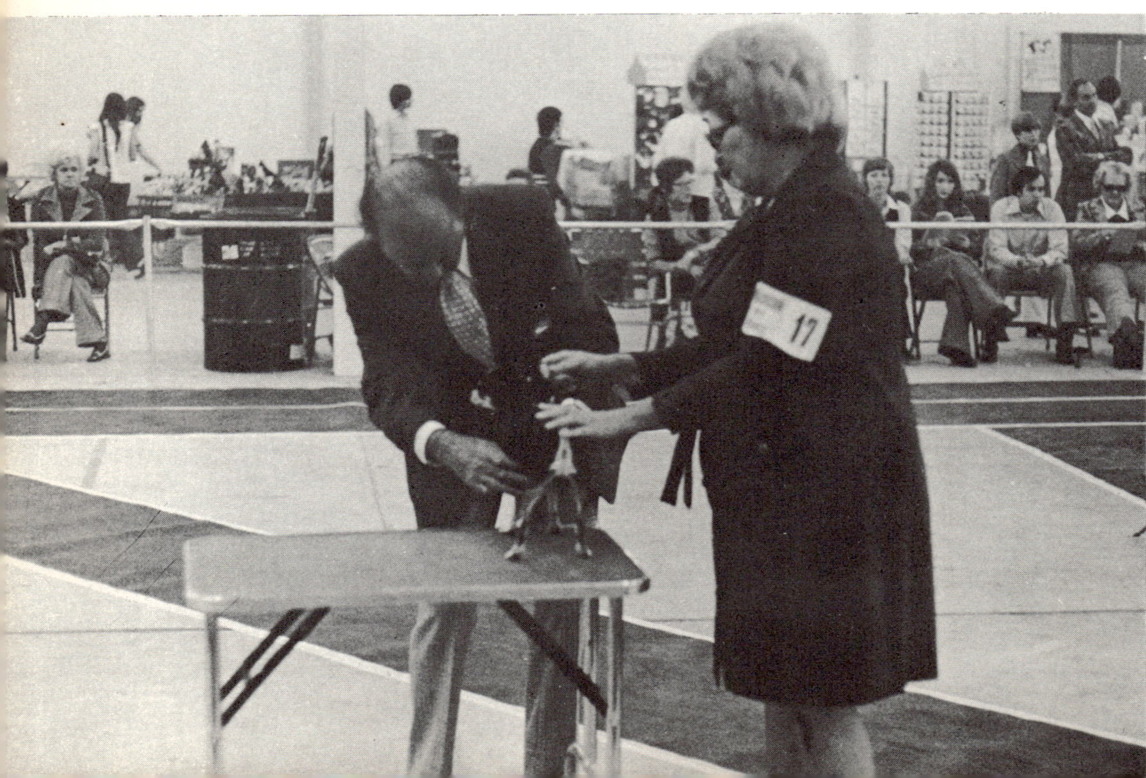

The handler stands at the side when posing the dog on the table for the judge's examination.

Placements

When the placements have been indicated by the judge, the winners should move directly to their numbers and should stand so that the judge can see armband numbers. This is a courtesy to the judge that even the most experienced exhibitor frequently forgets. The judge all too often has to walk the entire length of the line to ask to see armband numbers.

The exhibitor should practice to be both a gracious winner and a gracious loser. The winners should be congratulated and the judge should be thanked for the ribbon no matter what color it happens to be. An exhibitor has the right to ask the judge the reason for the dog's placement and judges usually give their opinions when asked. If he does not have time to give a full explanation during the judging, he may have time after finishing the class. When the judge gives his opinion, the handler should not challenge or dispute it. It is only an opinion, even though it may be based on years of experience either in judging the breed or in having raised it. If an exhibitor does not like a judge's opinion or he does not agree with it, he should not show that type dog under that particular judge again. The entry fee entitles an exhibitor to a fair examination and evaluation by a judge, but it does not guarantee a favorable decision from him. Wins should be accepted graciously and losses even more so.

It is not a wise action to catch a judge late in the day after the judging is over, or at the motel, and ask his opinion of your dog. He may well remember the dog but will be unable to remember that you were on the other end of the lead. The judge may have seen 175 dogs during the day. During the judging he concentrates on the dogs and not on the exhibitors and is most unlikely to remember which dog a particular handler showed him that day. Asking the judge such questions is unfair to him. There is also the possibility that the judge may identify the wrong dog with a particular handler and evaluate this dog instead.

Group line-up showing that each dog should be re-groomed whenever he is posed.

A dog badly posed will create faults that do not exist. Stretching the rear legs too far back and allowing the head to droop will cause the dog to roach his back. The exhibitor should watch his dog and not the camera.

In-Service Training

If time permits and an exhibitor is not showing other dogs that would cause a time conflict, he should stand at ringside to support the other exhibitors of the breed, thus learning new techniques in how to handle or, in some cases, how not to handle a dog. An exhibitor should watch the judge's ring procedure, especially before going into a ring under a judge for the first time. If one can watch him judge a different breed earlier in the day, one can determine his expected pattern for exhibitor behavior.

Many valuable lessons can be learned by watching other exhibitors show similar or, even in some cases, quite different breeds. Professional handlers can give invaluable lessons in showmanship and ring procedures. They know many special techniques for showing a dog to his fullest potential. Other invaluable information can come from long-established exhibitor-breeders, for they usually have a great deal of knowledge not found in books. Their knowledge is the result of years of trial and error and one should capitalize on this experience. All such information should, however, be weighed in relation to one's own breeding and showing program. Techniques that work under one set of circumstances may not necessarily work under another. With experience the exhibitor will learn to select the proper techniques for showing his dogs.

Doug Huffman and his well-posed Pug, Ch. Bonjour's Tuff Jorge'll Do It.